GLOBE EDUCATION
SHORTER SHAKESPEARE

SHAKESPEARE CENTRE LIBRARY
WITHDRAWN

TWELFTH NIGHT

- Get straight to the heart of the play
- Understand the whole story
- Read Shakespeare's language with confidence

HODDER
EDUCATION
AN HACHETTE UK COMPANY

Introduction

Shakespeare the writer

Shakespeare would probably be amazed that you are studying one of his plays in school over 400 years after his death. He did not write his plays to be read, he wrote them to be performed. When he wrote, he expected a company of skilful actors to interpret and perform his play for an audience to listen to and watch. He did not even have the script of *Twelfth Night* printed. It was first printed in 1623 (seven years after Shakespeare's death), in a collection of his plays known as the *First Folio*.

Prose and verse

Most of the time, Shakespeare wrote *blank verse* – verse where the ends of the lines do not rhyme. So what makes it verse? It has a rhythm. Normally there are ten syllables in every line. Shakespeare wrote the lines to be spoken with the stress on every second syllable. Try saying, "*baa-**boom** baa-**boom** baa-**boom** baa-**boom** baa-**boom***".

Moving on to a line from *Twelfth Night*, try saying it with the same rhythm and stress:

'*If **mu**–sic **be** – the **food** – of **love** – play **on***'.

Shakespeare can break the rules of blank verse, but he does not often do so in *Twelfth Night*. However, he does use a lot of prose instead of verse. Less socially important characters often speak in prose, as do comic characters. So Sir Toby and Sir Andrew speak in prose, as does the Fool, Feste. Olivia speaks in both prose and verse, depending on who she is speaking to. Orsino, on the other hand, speaks mainly in verse.

Shared lines: Sometimes Shakespeare had two characters share the ten syllables that make a line (as Cesario (Viola) and Orsino do on the right). He did this when he wanted the actors to keep the rhythm going. This was often to show the characters are particularly close, or when one is impatient.

Orsino	O then, unfold the passion of my love,	
	Surprise her with discourse of my dear faith.	
	It shall become thee well to act my woes.	20
	She will attend it better in thy youth	
	Than in a nuncio's of more grave aspect.	
Cesario (Viola)	I think not so, my lord.	
Orsino	Dear lad, believe it.	
	For they shall yet belie thy happy years	
	That say thou art a man. Diana's lip	25
	Is not more smooth and rubious, thy small pipe	
	Is as the maiden's organ, shrill and sound,	

Counting lines: You can see the number 20 at the end of the third line on the right. It is normal to print the line number every five lines in a Shakespeare play. This helps people find an exact place when talking or writing about the play. If you count, however, you will see there are six lines to line 25 – the two half-lines count as a single line.

How to use this book

Act and Scene: Printed plays are divided into Acts and Scenes. On the stage there is no real gap – a new scene happens when the story moves on, either to a new time or place. When Shakespeare's company performed indoors by candlelight they needed to trim the candles about every half an hour, so they picked points in the story where a short gap between scenes made sense. These became the divisions between Acts.

Elision: Elision is the correct term in English Literature for leaving a bit out. Shakespeare does it a lot. Often he cannot quite fit what he wants to say into his ten-syllable line, so he cheats – running two words together. In the highlighted examples, do not say *see it*, say *see't* (as you would say *seat*) – the inverted comma shows you there is something missing. Likewise, say *'tis* not *it is*, and run together *feel* and *it* so they sound like one word: *feel't*.

Act 4 Scene 3

Enter Sebastian.

Sebastian   This is the air; that is the glorious sun,
This pearl she gave me, I do feel't and see't,
And though 'tis wonder that enwraps me thus,
Yet 'tis not madness. Where's Antonio then?
I could not find him at the Elephant.   **5**

Stage Directions: Shakespeare wrote stage directions – mainly when characters enter or exit, but sometimes telling actors what to do. In this book we develop Shakespeare's stage directions a bit, to tell you what you would see if you were watching the play.

Some stage directions are in square brackets, we print them as part of an actor's lines. These help you understand who the actor is talking to – which would be obvious on stage. *Aside* is a significant one – this is when the character shares their thoughts with the audience.

Sir Toby   I'll make the motion. Stand here.
[To Cesario.] There's no remedy sir, he will fight with you for's oath' sake. He protests he will not hurt you.

Cesario (Viola) *[Aside.]* Pray God defend me! A little thing would   **155**
make me tell them how much I lack of a man.

152 the motion: the offer

154 for's oath' sake: because he swore to do so

The glossary: Some words and phrases have changed their meaning or fallen out of use since Shakespeare's time. The glossary helps you with them. It gives you the line numbers in the play (in red); then the word, or the start and end of a long phrase (with three dots to mark the elision where some words have been left out), in **bold**; then the explanation in modern English. It is as close to the original line as we can make it.

Orsino.
Look at his expression. Do you think when this photograph was taken he was describing music (lines 4–5), or Olivia (lines 29–30)? Explain the reason for your choice.

1   How do the words and images used by Orsino give a sense of sadness at the start of the play?
2   In Shakespeare's time, having music in your own home was only for the rich. What would the presence of music immediately tell the audience about Orsino?

The questions: There are questions in the photograph captions, and in red boxes. Here are two tips for answering them:

- There usually is not a simple 'right' answer. We hope you will develop your own ideas. The best way to answer any question is to be able to back up your answer with a reference to the play text.
- Unless we tell you otherwise, you can answer the question using the play text on the opposite page.

Heavens

Upper stage

Stage

Galleries

Entrances

Yard

The Globe Theatre

Today's *Shakespeare's Globe* in London was built to show us what open-air theatres were like in Shakespeare's time. It is very different from other modern theatres. Shakespeare wrote *Twelfth Night* for the original *Globe* theatre – so how was the play affected by the theatre it was written for?

- **The stage** was large, and stuck out into the audience, who surrounded it on three sides. The theatre was open-air, but a roof over the stage, called the Heavens, kept the actors (and their expensive costumes) dry if it rained. Two large pillars held up this roof, and the actors had to move around them.

- **The upper stage** was a balcony running along the back wall of the stage. Actors and musicians could use it. Also, it was the most expensive place for members of the audience to sit (showing off their fine clothes to the rest of the audience).

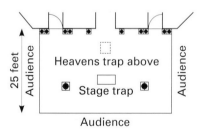

The stage trap opened into the area under the stage. The heavens trap was not on the stage, but above it. Actors playing gods might be lowered down to the stage through it.

Sam Wanamaker, an American actor and director, founded the Shakespeare's Globe Trust in 1970. Sam could not understand why there was not a proper memorial to the world's greatest playwright in the city where he had lived and worked. He started fundraising to build a new Globe Theatre. Sadly, Sam died before the theatre opened in 1997.

- **The entrances** were in the back wall of the stage, leading from the *Tiring House* (the actors' dressing room). There was a big door in the middle and a smaller door on either side. The big entrance was useful for bringing on large props like a bed or the table for Act 1 Scene 5.

- **Traps** allowed props or actors to appear or disappear from the Heavens or into the stage. The stage trap opened into the area under the stage. The Heavens trap was not on the stage, but above it, in the Heavens.

- **The audience** The theatre held well over 2,000 people (today's Globe holds 1,700). All the audience were close to the stage. People could pay a penny to stand in the open air in the Yard around the stage. Three tiers of roofed Galleries surrounded the Yard, where, for more money, people could sit on benches.

- **Sound, light and scenery** – there was not any, except for daylight, live music, and live sound effects (like rolling a cannonball in a trough to make a sound like thunder). The Globe was not dark, like a modern theatre; the actors and audience could all see each other – all the time. Shakespeare often started a play with a dramatic and noisy moment to grab the audience's attention. Characters often describe where they are, or say that it is dark – see the first two lines of Act 1 Scene 2 (page 9).

The full text of part of Act 1 Scene 2 (lines 6–27), showing the cuts in the *Shorter Shakespeare* text.

Captain	It is perchance that you yourself were saved.	
Viola	O my poor brother! And so perchance may he be.	
Captain	True madam. And to comfort you with chance,	
	Assure yourself. After our ship did split,	
	When you, and those poor number saved with you,	10
	Hung on our driving boat, I saw your brother,	
	~~Most provident in peril, bind himself~~	
	~~(Courage and hope both teaching him the practice)~~	
	~~To a strong mast that lived upon the sea.~~	
	~~Where, like Arion on the dolphin's back,~~	15
	I saw him hold acquaintance with the waves	
	So long as I could see.	
Viola	~~[Giving money] For saying so, there's gold.~~	
	~~Mine own escape unfoldeth to my hope,~~	
	~~Whereto thy speech serves for authority,~~	20
	~~The like of him.~~ Knowest thou this country?	
Captain	Ay madam, well, for I was bred and born	
	Not three hours' travel from this very place.	
Viola	Who governs here?	
Captain	A noble duke in nature, as in name.	25
Viola	What is his name?	
Captain	Orsino.	

What is 'Shorter Shakespeare'?

In the texts that survive, Shakespeare's plays are of very different lengths. The longest is 3,904 lines, and the shortest 1,918 lines (*Twelfth Night* is 2,579 lines). Plays were said to take about two hours in Shakespeare's time (3,900 lines would take about 4 hours), so his company must have *cut* the play for performance. This could have meant leaving out whole scenes, and/or shortening speeches throughout the play. Almost all productions of Shakespeare's plays ever since have made some cuts to the text.

Shorter Shakespeare cuts the play to help you study it in the classroom. Our cut is about 1,500 lines, and we have 'filleted' the text, so you get all the important parts. We do not add to, or change, the words – Shakespeare originally wrote them all. The example on the left shows you the sort of things we have cut (from Act 1 Scene 2).

...ino.

...k at his expression.
... you think when this
...otograph was taken
... was describing music
...es 4–5), or Olivia
...es 29–30)? Explain the
...ason for your choice.

1 How do the words and images used by Orsino give a sense of sadness at the start of the play?

2 In Shakespeare's time, having music in your own home was only for the rich. What would the presence of music immediately tell the audience about Orsino?

Act 1 Scene 1

Music is playing. Enter Duke Orsino, Curio, and other Lords.

Orsino   If music be the food of love, play on.
Give me excess of it, that surfeiting,
The appetite may sicken and so die.
That strain again, it had a dying fall.
O, it came o'er my ear like the sweet sound   5
That breathes upon a bank of violets,
Stealing and giving odour. Enough! No more!
'Tis not so sweet now as it was before.

The music stops.

O spirit of love, how quick and fresh art thou
That, notwithstanding thy capacity,   10
Receiveth as the sea. Naught enters there,
Of what validity and pitch soe'er,
But falls into abatement and low price
Even in a minute. So full of shapes is fancy
That it alone is high fantastical.   15
O when mine eyes did see Olivia first,
Methought she purged the air of pestilence.
That instant was I turned into a hart,
And my desires, like fell and cruel hounds,
E'er since pursue me.   *Enter Valentine.*
                    How now, what news from her?   20

Valentine   So please my lord, I might not be admitted,
But like a cloistress she will veilèd walk,
And water once a day her chamber round
With eye-offending brine. All this to season
A brother's dead love, which she would keep fresh   25
And lasting in her sad remembrance.

Orsino   O she that hath a heart of that fine frame
To pay this debt of love but to a brother,
How will she love, when liver, brain, and heart,
These sovereign thrones, are all supplied and filled   30
(Her sweet perfections!) with one selfsame king.
Away before me, to sweet beds of flowers,
Love thoughts lie rich when canopied with bowers.

They all exit.

2 **that:** so that
2 **surfeiting:** over-indulging
3 **appetite:** hunger for it
4 **That strain again:** play that part again
4 **dying fall:** falling rhythm
9 **quick:** lively
9 **fresh:** vigorous
10–11 **notwithstanding thy … sea:** whatever your size, can hold any amount
11 **Naught:** nothing
12 **Of what validity … soe'er:** whatever its value or quality
13 **falls into … price:** loses value
14 **shapes:** images
14 **fancy:** love
15 **is high fantastical:** stretches imagination most
17 **purged:** cleaned
17 **pestilence:** disease
18 **hart:** male deer [a pun on 'heart']
19 **fell:** ruthless, fierce
20 **e'er:** ever
21 **I might … admitted:** I was not allowed in
22 **cloistress:** nun
24 **eye-offending brine:** salty tears
24 **season:** preserve [meat was preserved in salt]
26 **remembrance:** memory
27 **of that fine frame:** so well made
28 **but to:** simply for
29–30 **liver, brain … thrones:** the liver was said to rule passion; the brain, reason and the heart, emotion
31 **one selfsame:** a single
33 **canopied with bowers:** in a sheltered garden spot

Viola, after the shipwreck, with the Captain (hatless) and two sailors. Which word best describes Viola in this photograph: *proud*, *vulnerable*, *defiant*?

1 How does the language used by the Captain help the audience to form an impression of Olivia and Orsino?

2 What impression do you have of Viola from her first appearance in this scene? Think about the way she decides to disguise herself and the way she plans to serve Orsino.

Boys playing girls (playing boys)

In Shakespeare's time, women were not allowed to act in public theatres. Boys and men played all the parts. An acting company would include experienced actors and boys learning their trade as apprentices. Leading female roles, such as Viola and Olivia in *Twelfth Night*, were played by boy actors whose voices had not yet broken. Some older men specialised in playing older women; sometimes seriously, sometimes in a comic style, making them seem silly.

Many comedies of the time had plots that included girls disguising themselves as boys. Shakespeare did this in several of his plays, including *As You Like It* and *Two Gentlemen of Verona*. So when Viola says to the Captain: 'Conceal me what I am (line 36)' the audience was ready for some comic confusion, possibly made more amusing because the actor really was a boy.

Act 1 Scene 2

Enter Viola, a Captain, and Sailors.

Viola	What country, friends, is this?
Captain	This is Illyria, lady.
Viola	And what should I do in Illyria?
	My brother he is in Elysium.
	Perchance he is not drowned. What think you, sailors? 5
Captain	It is perchance that you yourself were saved.
Viola	O my poor brother! And so perchance may he be.
Captain	True madam. And to comfort you with chance,
	Assure yourself. After our ship did split,
	When you, and those poor number saved with you, 10
	Hung on our driving boat, I saw your brother,
	I saw him hold acquaintance with the waves
	So long as I could see.
Viola	Knowest thou this country?
Captain	Ay madam, well, for I was bred and born 15
	Not three hours' travel from this very place.
Viola	Who governs here?
Captain	A noble duke in nature, as in name.
Viola	What is his name?
Captain	Orsino. 20
Viola	Orsino? I have heard my father name him.
	He was a bachelor then.
Captain	And so is now, or was so very late.
	For but a month ago I went from hence,
	And then 'twas fresh in murmur 25
	That he did seek the love of fair Olivia.
Viola	What's she?
Captain	A virtuous maid, the daughter of a count
	That died some twelvemonth since, then leaving her
	In the protection of his son, her brother, 30
	Who shortly also died. For whose dear love
	(They say) she hath abjured the sight
	And company of men.
Viola	There is a fair behaviour in thee captain,
	I prithee (and I'll pay thee bounteously) 35
	Conceal me what I am, and be my aid
	For such disguise as haply shall become
	The form of my intent. I'll serve this duke.
	What else may hap, to time I will commit.
	Only shape thou thy silence to my wit. 40
	Lead me on. *They both exit.*

4 Elysium: Heaven in Greek myths [so he is dead]
5 Perchance: [here] perhaps
6 perchance: [here] by lucky chance
7 perchance: [in both senses]
8 chance: the possibility of good luck
9 Assure yourself: you need to know this
10 poor number: few
11 driving: storm-driven
12 hold acquaintance with: befriended by
14 Ay: yes
23 late: recently
24 hence: here
25 fresh in murmur: newly rumoured
32 abjured: withdrawn from
35 I prithee: Please ['I pray you']
34 bounteously: generously
36 Conceal me what I am: help me disguise myself
37–8 haply shall … my intent: will suit my plans
39 hap: happen
40 Only shape … my wit: Just follow my plan

Waiting gentlewoman

Maria is Olivia's *waiting gentlewoman*. She was neither completely a servant, nor completely part of the family. Waiting gentlewomen served grand and noble ladies. They were servants, but more important than the servants who cleaned or cooked. They were usually a few steps less important than the lady they served. So Queen Elizabeth's waiting gentlewomen came from the most important families in the country. These women had waiting gentlewomen too, from less important families.

A waiting gentlewoman helped her lady to dress, did her hair and kept her company. She might read to her lady, play music to her, or write letters for her. She talked to her lady and also kept her secrets.

Sir Toby and Maria (from a modern-dress production). She is replacing his bottle of champagne with a cup of water (without him noticing). What does this photograph suggest about the characters of Maria and Sir Toby, and the relationship between them?

Act 1 Scene 3

Enter Sir Toby and Maria.

Sir Toby	What a plague means my niece to take the death of her brother thus? I am sure care's an enemy to life.
Maria	By my troth Sir Toby, you must come in earlier a-nights. Your cousin, my lady, takes great exceptions to your ill hours. 5
Sir Toby	Why let her except, before excepted.
Maria	That quaffing and drinking will undo you. I heard my lady talk of it yesterday, and of a foolish knight that you brought in one night here to be her wooer.
Sir Toby	Who, Sir Andrew Aguecheek? 10
Maria	Ay, he.
Sir Toby	He's as tall a man as any's in Illyria.
Maria	What's that to th' purpose? He's a very fool and a prodigal.
Sir Toby	Fie, that you'll say so! He speaks three or four languages 15 word for word without book, and hath all the good gifts of nature.
Maria	He hath indeed all, most natural, for, besides that he's a fool, he's a great quarreller.
Sir Toby	By this hand, they are scoundrels and substractors 20 that say so of him. Who are they?
Maria	They that add, moreover, he's drunk nightly in your company.
Sir Toby	With drinking healths to my niece. I'll drink to her as long as there is a passage in my throat and drink in 25 Illyria.

Enter Sir Andrew Aguecheek.

	Here comes Sir Andrew Agueface.
Sir Andrew	Sir Toby Belch! How now, Sir Toby Belch?
Sir Toby	Sweet Sir Andrew.
Sir Andrew	*[To Maria.]* Bless you fair shrew. 30
Maria	And you too, sir.
Sir Toby	*[To Sir Andrew.]* Accost, Sir Andrew, accost.
Sir Andrew	*[To Sir Toby.]* What's that?
Sir Toby	*[To Sir Andrew.]* My niece's chambermaid.
Sir Andrew	*[To Maria.]* Good Mistress Accost, I desire better 35 acquaintance.
Maria	My name is Mary, sir.

---

1 What a plague: an oath similar to the modern 'What the hell'

2 care: worry

3 By my troth: Honestly

4 cousin: used for any close relative at the time

4–5 takes great … ill hours: dislikes you being out so late

6 let her … excepted: [playing with the word 'exception', not taking the situation seriously]

7 quaffing and drinking: drinking such huge amounts

7 undo you: be the ruin of you

12 any's: any man is

13 What's that … purpose?: What's your point?

14 a prodigal: wildly extravagant

15 Fie: used to reproach someone for something said or done

16 without book: from memory

18 natural: like an idiot

20 By this hand: a mild oath

20 substractors: [drunken missaying of 'detractors': slanderers]

30 shrew: a small mouse or a bad tempered woman

32 Accost: several meanings [punned on after]: approach [sexually], greet, woo, board

34 chambermaid: ladies' maid

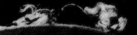

Viola, disguised as Cesario.
Look back to the photograph on page 8.
What has changed and what has stayed
the same?

Sir Andrew	Good Mistress Mary Accost—
Sir Toby	You mistake knight. "Accost" is front her, board her, woo her, assail her.	40
Sir Andrew	*[To Sir Toby.]* By my troth I would not undertake her in this company. Is that the meaning of "accost"?
Maria	Fare you well, gentlemen.

Exit Maria.

Sir Toby	O knight, when did I see thee so put down?
Sir Andrew	I'll ride home tomorrow, Sir Toby.	45
Sir Toby	*Pourquoi*, my dear knight?
Sir Andrew	What is "*pourquoi*"? Do, or not do? O had I but followed the arts! Your niece will not be seen, or if she be, it's four to one she'll none of me. The Count himself here hard by woos her.	50
Sir Toby	She'll none o' th' Count. She'll not match above her degree, neither in estate, years, nor wit. I have heard her swear't. Tut, there's life in't man.
Sir Andrew	I'll stay a month longer. Shall we set about some revels?
Sir Toby	What shall we do else? Let me see thee caper.	55

[Sir Andrew dances.] Ha, higher! Ha, ha, excellent!

They exit.

Act 1 Scene 4

Enter Valentine, and Viola (disguised as Cesario, a young man).

| Valentine | If the Duke continue these favours towards you Cesario, you are like to be much advanced. He hath known you but three days, and already you are no stranger. |

Enter Orsino, Curio, and Attendants.

Orsino	Who saw Cesario, ho?
Cesario (Viola)	On your attendance, my lord, here.	5
Orsino	*[To Curio and Attendants.]* Stand you awhile aloof. *[They move away.]* Cesario, Thou know'st no less but all. I have unclasped To thee the book even of my secret soul. Therefore, good youth, address thy gait unto her. Be not denied access, stand at her doors	10
	And tell them there thy fixèd foot shall grow Till thou have audience.
Cesario (Viola)	Sure, my noble lord, If she be so abandoned to her sorrow As it is spoke, she never will admit me.

41 undertake: make sexual advances to
42 in this company: in front of others

44 put down: silenced, drunk

46 *Pourquoi*: why [French]

50 hard by: nearby
51 match: marry
52 degree: social status
52 estate: wealth
52 wit: intelligence
53 there's life in't: there's still hope
54 set about some revels: enjoy ourselves
55 else: otherwise
55 caper: dance

What's just happened

- Viola, shipwrecked on Illyria, has disguised herself as a young man to serve Duke Orsino.
- She calls herself Cesario. No one at the court knows she is a woman.

How is Viola feeling at this point?

2 advanced: promoted
3 but: only
3 you are no stranger: he tells you everything
6 aloof: aside
7 no less but all: everything
9 address thy gait: go
12 thou shall have audience: she will see you
13 abandoned to: absorbed by
14 spoke: rumoured

A

Orsino and Cesario (Viola in disguise). These photographs were taken between lines 25 and 34. They are not in the order they were taken in (i.e. A was not the first one taken). What is the right order?

B

1 How do the words Orsino uses to explain to Cesario (Viola) that he (she) should not be turned away from Olivia's house show the audience how desperate Orsino is to gain Olivia's love?

2 How is the theme of love developed in this scene? Think about Cesario's (Viola's) words at the end of the scene.

C

Asides

Asides are lines spoken by a character that some (or all) of the other people on stage cannot hear. Shakespeare often uses them to show the audience what the character is really thinking.

Orsino	Be clamorous and leap all civil bounds	**15**
	Rather than make unprofited return.	
Cesario (Viola)	Say I do speak with her my lord, what then?	
Orsino	O then, unfold the passion of my love,	
	Surprise her with discourse of my dear faith.	
	It shall become thee well to act my woes.	**20**
	She will attend it better in thy youth	
	Than in a nuncio's of more grave aspect.	
Cesario (Viola)	I think not so, my lord.	
Orsino	Dear lad, believe it.	
	For they shall yet belie thy happy years	
	That say thou art a man. Diana's lip	**25**
	Is not more smooth and rubious, thy small pipe	
	Is as the maiden's organ, shrill and sound,	
	And all is semblative a woman's part.	
	I know thy constellation is right apt	
	For this affair. — Prosper well in this	**30**
	And thou shalt live as freely as thy lord,	
	To call his fortunes thine.	
Cesario (Viola)	I'll do my best	
	To woo your lady. *[Aside.]* Yet a barful strife!	
	Whoe'er I woo, myself would be his wife.	

They all exit.

Act 1 Scene 5

Enter Maria and Feste.

Maria	Nay, either tell me where thou hast been, or my lady will hang thee for thy absence.	
Feste	Let her hang me. He that is well hanged in this world needs to fear no colours.	
Maria	Yet you will be hanged for being so long absent, or to be turned away. Is not that as good as a hanging to you?	**5**
Feste	Many a good hanging prevents a bad marriage.	
Maria	You are resolute then?	
Feste	Not so, neither, but I am resolved on two points.	
Maria	That if one break, the other will hold, or if both break, your gaskins fall.	**10**
Feste	Apt, in good faith, very apt. Well, go thy way. If Sir Toby would leave drinking, thou wert as witty a piece of Eve's flesh as any in Illyria.	
Maria	Peace, you rogue. no more o' that. Here comes my lady. Make your excuse wisely, you were best. *She exits.*	**15**

15 leap all civil bounds: be pushy, not polite

16 make unprofited return: come back without seeing her

19 Surprise: ambush

19 discourse: speaking

19 faith: faithful love

21 in thy: of your

22 nuncio: messenger

22 grave aspect: serious manner

24 belie: misrepresent

25 Diana: Roman goddess of the moon, hunting and virginity

26 rubious: ruby red

26 pipe: voice

28 is semblative: resembles

29 thy constellation: your stars

29 right apt: entirely suitable

30 Prosper well: succeed

32 To call: You'll be able to call

33 barful strife: conflict-ridden task

34 Whoe'er I woo: the person I'm wooing for

3 well hanged: [sexual pun]

4 fear no colours: fear nothing [a military phrase - the enemy's flags]

6 turned away: dismissed, sacked

9 points: double meaning: 1) talking points; 2) ties to hold breeches up

11 gaskins: breeches

13 leave: give up

13–14 piece of Eve's flesh: woman

16 you were best: that's my advice

Olivia and Malvolio.
What do the costumes and props suggest about who is the most powerful?

1 This scene is the first time that the audience sees Malvolio. How would you tell the actor playing Malvolio to behave towards Olivia?

2 How does the language he uses about Feste suggest Malvolio should behave towards Feste?

Fools

Fools were employed to entertain royal and noble families. They were expected to speak or act foolishly, using puns, irony, or simply speaking nonsense. Unlike other members of court, fools were allowed to mock their masters and mistresses and bluntly speak the truth. In plays, fools and other comic parts were played by actors who specialised in these roles. There were different styles of this clowning. Will Kemp (clown for Shakespeare's company in the 1590s) was a much more physical comic than his successor Robert Armin (who joined the company in about 1600). Kemp was famous for his jigs and dancing. Armin's comedy was more verbal and musical; he was a good singer and ventriloquist.

Feste falls into the category of 'wise fool' who could ridicule others using his wit and trickery. He was also allowed to speak very bluntly, as he does with Olivia in this scene. Feste's comedy reflects Armin's skills, for example his double roles as Feste and Sir Topas in Act 4 Scene 2.

Enter Lady Olivia with Malvolio and attendants.

Feste	God bless thee lady.
Olivia	Take the Fool away.
Feste	Do you not hear, fellows? Take away the Lady.
Olivia	Go to, you're a dry Fool. I'll no more of you.
Feste	Good madonna, give me leave to prove you a fool.
Olivia	Can you do it?
Feste	Dexteriously, good madonna.
Olivia	Make your proof.
Feste	Good madonna, why mourn'st thou?
Olivia	Good Fool, for my brother's death.
Feste	I think his soul is in hell, madonna.
Olivia	I know his soul is in heaven, Fool.
Feste	The more fool, madonna, to mourn for your brother's soul, being in heaven. Take away the fool, gentlemen.
Olivia	What think you of this Fool, Malvolio?
Malvolio	I marvel your Ladyship takes delight in such a barren rascal. I saw him put down the other day with an ordinary fool, that has no more brain than a stone.
Olivia	O you are sick of self-love Malvolio, and taste with a distempered appetite.

Enter Maria.

Maria	Madam, there is at the gate a young gentleman much desires to speak with you.
Olivia	From the Count Orsino, is it?
Maria	I know not, madam. 'Tis a fair young man, and well attended.
Olivia	Who of my people hold him in delay?
Maria	Sir Toby, madam, your kinsman.
Olivia	Fetch him off, I pray you. He speaks nothing but madman. Fie on him! *Maria exits.* Go you, Malvolio. If it be a suit from the Count, I am sick, or not at home — what you will, to dismiss it. *Malvolio exits.* [*To Feste.*] Now you see sir, how your fooling grows old, and people dislike it.
Feste	Thou hast spoke for us, madonna, as if thy eldest son should be a Fool.

Enter Sir Toby.

Olivia	By mine honour, half drunk. What is he at the gate, cousin?

Line numbers (right margin): 20, 25, 30, 35, 40, 45, 50

20 Go to: that's enough of this
20 dry: dull
21 madonna: my lady

23 Dexteriously: skilfully

32 barren: lacking wit, unproductive
33 with: by

36 distempered: unbalanced

40–1 well attended: with several servants
42 hold him in delay: is with him while he waits

44 Fetch him off: Get him out of the way
44–5 he speaks … madman: he's talking gibberish
46 suit: plea of love
47 what you will: whatever you think best
48 grows old: gets boring

Viola (disguised as Cesario) from a modern-dress production.
Inset: Viola as she appeared in the shipwreck scene in the same production.
How has the director changed her appearance? How effective do you think this is?

Sir Toby	A gentleman.
Olivia	A gentleman? What gentleman? 55
Sir Toby	'Tis a gentleman here, *[He belches.]* — a plague o' these pickle herring! *[To Feste.]* How now, sot?
Feste	Good Sir Toby.
Olivia	Cousin, cousin, how have you come so early by this lethargy? 60
Sir Toby	Lechery? I defy lechery. There's one at the gate.
Olivia	Ay, marry, what is he?
Sir Toby	Let him be the devil an he will, I care not. Give me faith, say I. Well, it's all one. *He exits.*
Olivia	What's a drunken man like, Fool? 65
Feste	Like a drowned man, a fool, and a madman. One draught above heat makes him a fool, the second mads him, and a third drowns him.
Olivia	He's in the third degree of drink: he's drowned. Go look after him. 70
Feste	He is but mad yet, madonna, and the Fool shall look to the madman. *He exits.*

Enter Malvolio.

Malvolio	Madam, yond young fellow swears he will speak with you. I told him you were sick, he takes on him to understand so much, and therefore comes to speak 75 with you. What is to be said to him, lady? He's fortified against any denial.
Olivia	What kind o' man is he?
Malvolio	Why, of mankind.
Olivia	What manner of man? 80
Malvolio	Of very ill manner. He'll speak with you, will you or no.
Olivia	Of what personage and years is he?
Malvolio	Not yet old enough for a man, nor young enough for a boy. One would think his mother's milk were scarce out of him. 85
Olivia	Let him approach. Call in my gentlewoman.
Malvolio	Gentlewoman, my lady calls. *He exits.*

Enter Maria.

Olivia	Give me my veil. Come, throw it o'er my face. We'll once more hear Orsino's embassy.

Enter Cesario (Viola disguised as a man).

Cesario (Viola)	The honourable lady of the house, which is she? 90

---

57 sot: drunkard

60 lethargy: drunken, dozy, state
61 lechery: sexual desire [he has misheard 'lethargy']

63 an: if

66–7 one draught above heat: one drink more than enough to warm him

71 look to: look after

73 yond: that
74–5 takes on … so much: assures me he understands this
76–7 he's fortified … denial: he just won't take no for an answer

79 of mankind: ordinary
80 What manner of man: What's he like
81 of very ill manner: very rude
82 personage: appearance

89 embassy: messenger

Olivia (from a modern-dress production).
Which line do you think was being spoken when this photograph was taken: 100, 103, or 121–2?

Olivia	Speak to me, I shall answer for her. Your will?
Cesario (Viola)	Most radiant, exquisite, and unmatchable beauty — I pray you, tell me if this be the lady of the house, for I never saw her.
Olivia	Whence came you, sir? 95
Cesario (Viola)	I can say little more than I have studied, and that question's out of my part. Good gentle one, give me modest assurance, if you be the lady of the house, that I may proceed in my speech.
Olivia	Are you a comedian? 100
Cesario (Viola)	No, my profound heart. And yet, I swear I am not that I play. Are you the lady of the house?
Olivia	I am.
Cesario (Viola)	I will on with my speech in your praise, and then show you the heart of my message. 105
Olivia	Come to what is important in't. I forgive you the praise.
Cesario (Viola)	It alone concerns your ear.
Olivia	What are you? What would you?
Cesario (Viola)	What I am, and what I would, are as secret as maidenhead: to your ears, divinity; to any other's, 110 profanation.
Olivia	Give us the place alone, we will hear this divinity.
	Maria and Attendants exit.
	Now, sir, what is your text?
Cesario (Viola)	Most sweet lady —
Olivia	A comfortable doctrine, and much may be said of it. 115 Where lies your text?
Cesario (Viola)	In Orsino's bosom.
Olivia	O, I have read it, it is heresy. Have you no more to say?
Cesario (Viola)	Good madam, let me see your face.
Olivia	Have you any commission from your lord to negotiate 120 with my face? You are now out of your text. But we will draw the curtain and show you the picture. *[Unveiling.]* Look you sir, such a one I was this present. Is't not well done?
Cesario (Viola)	Excellently done, if God did all. 125
Olivia	'Tis in grain sir, 'twill endure wind and weather.
Cesario (Viola)	Lady, you are the cruel'st she alive If you will lead these graces to the grave And leave the world no copy.
Olivia	O sir, I will not be so hard-hearted. I will give out 130 divers schedules of my beauty. It shall be inventoried

91 **Your will?:** What do you want?

95 **Whence:** from where
96 **studied:** memorised
97 **out of my part:** not in my script
98 **modest:** reasonable

100 **comedian:** actor
101 **my profound heart:** I swear it
101 **that:** the person that

106 **forgive you:** excuse you from

108 **What would you?:** What do you want?
110 **maidenhead:** virginity
110 **divinity:** holy words
111 **profanation:** blasphemy
112 **Give us … alone:** leave us

113 **your text:** the topic of you sermon [she then uses religious language]

115 **comfortable doctrine:** comforting belief
116 **your text:** the subject of your speech
118 **heresy:** false religious teaching

120 **commission:** instruction
120 **out of your text:** straying from your script
123 **Such a one … present:** this is what I look like
125 **if God did all:** if it's natural – not make-up
126 **in grain:** won't wash off

129 **leave the world no copy:** don't have children

131 **divers schedules:** various lists
131 **inventoried:** listed one by one

21

A

Olivia.
Do you think these photographs were taken before or after Cesario exits?

Courtship

In Shakespeare's time, marriages, especially in important families, were usually arranged by the families, based on wealth and social importance. A father chose a husband for his daughter, or a man might ask a father for permission to woo. A key person was the go-between – who wooed one person on the other person's behalf. The go-between then delivered messages and gifts between the couple, as Cesario (Viola disguised as a young man) was sent to Olivia by Orsino. This tradition was starting to shift towards marriages based on mutual affection.

B

3 How does the language Cesario (Viola) uses in the speech beginning '*Make me a willow cabin…*' (line 150) show the power of her developing feelings of love?

22

	and every particle and utensil labelled: as, *item* two lips indifferent red, *item* two gray eyes, with lids to them, *item* one neck, one chin, and so forth. Were you sent hither to praise me?	135
Cesario (Viola)	I see you what you are, you are too proud. But, if you were the devil, you are fair. My lord and master loves you.	
Olivia	How does he love me?	
Cesario (Viola)	With adorations, fertile tears, With groans that thunder love, with sighs of fire.	140
Olivia	Your lord does know my mind, I cannot love him. Yet I suppose him virtuous, know him noble, A gracious person. But yet I cannot love him. He might have took his answer long ago.	145
Cesario (Viola)	If I did love you in my master's flame, With such a suff'ring, such a deadly life, In your denial, I would find no sense, I would not understand it.	
Olivia	Why, what would you?	
Cesario (Viola)	Make me a willow cabin at your gate, And call upon my soul within the house, Write loyal cantons of contemnèd love, And sing them loud even in the dead of night. Halloo your name to the reverberate hills And make the babbling gossip of the air Cry out "Olivia!" O, you should not rest Between the elements of air and earth But you should pity me.	150 155
Olivia	You might do much. What is your parentage?	
Cesario (Viola)	Above my fortunes, yet my state is well. I am a gentleman.	160
Olivia	Get you to your lord. I cannot love him. Let him send no more, Unless (perchance) you come to me again To tell me how he takes it. Fare you well. I thank you for your pains. Spend this for me.	165
Cesario (Viola)	I am no fee'd post, lady. Keep your purse, My master, not myself, lacks recompense. Farewell, fair cruelty. *He exits.*	
Olivia	"What is your parentage?" "Above my fortunes, yet my state is well. I am a gentleman." I'll be sworn thou art.	170

135 hither: here

137 But, if: but even if

140 fertile: abundant

143 suppose him: assume he is

145 took: accepted

146 in my master's flame: with my master's passion
147 deadly: death-like

149 what would you?: what would you do?

150 willow cabin: shelter of willow branches [willows were symbols of love not returned]
151 my soul: [i.e. Olivia]
152 cantons: songs
152 contemnèd: rejected
154 reverberate: echoing
155 babbling … the air: refers to the Greek myth of Echo who pined away for love of Narcissus, leaving only her echoing voice
157 elements: the elements were: earth, air, fire and water
160 above my fortunes: better than my present position suggests

165 Spend this for me: [tries to give him money]
166 fee'd post: paid messenger
167 recompense: payment for his effort

23

Olivia and Malvolio.
Compare the Olivia and Malvolio in this production with the ones from the original-dress production (page 16). What are the similarities?

4 How do Olivia's words at the end of this scene, where she describes her reactions to Cesario (Viola), emphasise the powerful impact of love on people?

Social status

Shakespeare wrote about a very class-conscious world. Orsino and Olivia are both aristocrats, but his family are more important than hers. Normally, families were run by a man. He was the 'head of the household' (all the family plus their servants). Wealthy and important people did not run their own house and lands; a steward did this for them. He was the most important servant in a household, controlling the spending and making the household run smoothly. In *Twelfth Night*, Olivia's father and brother are dead. She is unmarried, so, unusually, she is the head of the household (until she marries, when her husband will take over). Her steward (Malvolio) has to guide her through this responsibility.

Not everybody from an upper-class family was rich – Sir Toby probably lives in Olivia's household to save money. Maria, Olivia's waiting gentlewoman, probably grew up in an upper-class family, but has no money of her own. She is not as important as Malvolio, but is more important than the other servants.

Thy tongue, thy face, thy limbs, actions, and spirit
Do give thee fivefold blazon. Not too fast! Soft, soft,
Even so quickly may one catch the plague?
Methinks I feel this youth's perfections   **175**
With an invisible and subtle stealth
To creep in at mine eyes. Well, let it be. —
What ho, Malvolio!

173 blazon: gentleman's coat of arms
174 catch the plague: fall in love

Enter Malvolio.

Malvolio   Here madam, at your service.

Olivia   Run after that same peevish messenger,   **180**
The County's man. He left this ring behind him,
Would I or not. Tell him I'll none of it.
Desire him not to flatter with his lord,
Nor hold him up with hopes, I am not for him.
If that the youth will come this way tomorrow,   **185**
I'll give him reasons for't. Hie thee, Malvolio.

180 peevish: headstrong
181 The County's: Orsino's
182 Would I or not: whether I wanted it or not
182 I'll none of it: I don't want it
183 flatter with: encourage
186 Hie thee: hurry up

Malvolio   Madam, I will.   *He exits.*

Olivia   I do I know not what, and fear to find
Mine eye too great a flatterer for my mind.
Fate, show thy force, ourselves we do not owe,   **190**
What is decreed, must be. And be this so.   *She exits.*

189 Mine eye … my mind: his good looks may have affected my judgement
190 force: strength, power
190 owe: own
191 decreed: decided by fate

These questions ask you to reflect on all of Act 1

a) How does the language used by Orsino during Act 1 show how he seems to wallow in his unrequited love for Olivia?

b) How important is the idea of formal courtship which existed in Shakespeare's time in understanding the way Orsino and Olivia behave towards each other?

c) How is the theme of love developed during Act 1?

d) How should the actor playing Viola change her performance as she becomes Cesario during Act 1?

e) What impression do you form of Olivia's servants Maria, Malvolio and Feste during Act 1?

Sebastian and Antonio.
Which do you think is which?
Explain your answer.

Act 2 Scene 1

Enter Antonio and Sebastian.

Antonio	Will you stay no longer? Nor will you not that I go with you?
Sebastian	By your patience, no.
Antonio	Let me yet know of you whither you are bound.
Sebastian	No, sooth, sir. My determinate voyage is mere extravagancy. But I perceive in you so excellent a touch of modesty that you will not extort from me what I am willing to keep in. Therefore it charges me in manners the rather to express myself. You must know of me then, Antonio, my name is Sebastian, which I called Roderigo. My father was that Sebastian of Messaline whom I know you have heard of. He left behind him myself and a sister, both born in an hour. If the heavens had been pleased, would we had so ended. But you sir, altered that, for some hour before you took me from the breach of the sea, was my sister drowned.
Antonio	Alas the day!
Sebastian	A lady, sir, though it was said she much resembled me, was yet of many accounted beautiful. She is drowned already, sir, with salt water, though I seem to drown her remembrance again with more.
Antonio	If you will not murder me for my love, let me be your servant.
Sebastian	If you will not undo what you have done (that is, kill him whom you have recovered) desire it not. Fare ye well at once. I am bound to the Count Orsino's court. Farewell. *He exits.*
Antonio	The gentleness of all the gods go with thee. I have many enemies in Orsino's court, Else would I very shortly see thee there. But come what may, I do adore thee so That danger shall seem sport, and I will go. *He exits.*

Line numbers: 5, 10, 15, 20, 25, 30

Glossary:

1–2 **Nor will … with you?:** And you don't want me to go with you?

3 **By your patience:** if you don't mind

4 **whither:** where

4 **bound:** going

5 **sooth:** in truth

5–6 **My determinate … extravagancy:** I plan to just wander around

7 **modesty:** good manners

8–9 **it charges … express myself:** it's only polite that I tell you who I really am

13 **both born in an hour:** born in the same hour [twins]

13–4 **If the heavens … so ended:** if only our stars had let us die then

16 **breach of the sea:** tossing waves

19 **of many:** by many

21 **remembrance:** memory

21 **more:** [i.e. tears]

22 **If you will … my love:** If you don't want me to die of a broken heart

25 **recovered:** saved [from drowning]

30 **Else:** otherwise

32 **sport:** a game

1 Antonio's final speech in this scene is in verse. Looking at what Antonio says, why do you think this part of the scene is in verse and not prose?

2 It is clear from his words that Antonio likes Sebastian very much. How should an actor playing Antonio move and speak in this scene?

3 When the play was written, life was more dangerous than it is now. How would an audience in Shakespeare's time feel about Sebastian saying Antonio cannot follow him in order to protect him in this new country?

4 How do Antonio's words in this scene add to the idea of love in the play?

5 What sort of person is Sebastian shown to be in this scene? Think about what he tells Antonio about his past life.

Rings

In Shakespeare's time, men and women gave each other rings as a special sign of love, gratitude or friendship. Rings were often given during courtship, or on marriage, and their value was greater than the cost of buying them – because of the feelings of the person who gave the ring and the person who accepted it.

Important people might send each other rings by messenger. If so, the messenger usually gave the ring openly, with a message from the giver. Olivia doesn't do this. She sends Malvolio to give Cesario (Viola in disguise) a ring to show her love, but pretends she is returning a ring sent to her by Orsino.

Cesario and Malvolio.
Malvolio is holding the ring Olivia gave him to 'return' to Cesario. Which line was being spoken when this photograph was taken?

1 How does the language used in this scene emphasise the uncertainty and confusion caused by Viola's disguise?

2 How do Cesario's (Viola's) words in this scene show the dangers of pretending to be someone you are not?

3 How do Cesario's (Viola's) actions and words in this scene show that she is very observant and able to understand what is happening around her?

Act 2 Scene 2

Enter Cesario (Viola disguised as a man), and Malvolio, at different doors.

Malvolio   Were not you even now with the Countess Olivia?

Cesario (Viola) Even now sir.

Malvolio   She returns this ring to you, sir. You might have saved
me my pains to have taken it away yourself. She adds,
moreover, that you should put your lord into a   5
desperate assurance, she will none of him.

Cesario (Viola) She took the ring of me, I'll none of it.

Malvolio   Come sir, you peevishly threw it to her, and her will is
it should be so returned. *[Throwing down the ring.]*
If it be worth stooping for, there it lies, in your eye, if   10
not, be it his that finds it.   *He exits.*

Cesario (Viola) *[Picking up the ring.]*
I left no ring with her. What means this lady?
Fortune forbid my outside have not charmed her.
She made good view of me, indeed so much
That methought her eyes had lost her tongue,   15
For she did speak in starts, distractedly.
She loves me sure! The cunning of her passion
Invites me in this churlish messenger.
None of my lord's ring? Why, he sent her none!
I am the man! If it be so, as 'tis,   20
Poor lady, she were better love a dream.
Disguise, I see thou art a wickedness
Wherein the pregnant enemy does much.
How easy is it for the proper false
In women's waxen hearts to set their forms.   25
Alas, our frailty is the cause, not we,
For such as we are made of, such we be.
How will this fadge? My master loves her dearly,
And I, poor monster, fond as much on him,
And she (mistaken) seems to dote on me.   30
What will become of this? As I am man,
My state is desperate for my master's love.
As I am woman (now, alas the day)
What thriftless sighs shall poor Olivia breathe?
O Time, thou must untangle this, not I.   35
It is too hard a knot for me t' untie.   *She exits.*

1   **even now:** just now

4   **my pains:** the bother
4   **to have taken:** if you had taken
5–6 **put your lord … assurance:** make you lord understand the hopelessness of his position

8   **peevishly:** rudely

13   **my outside:** my appearance
14   **made good view of me:** certainly looked me over
15   **had lost her tongue:** had made her lose her tongue
16   **in starts:** in bursts
16   **distractedly:** madly
18   **in:** by
18   **churlish:** rude
21   **were better love:** would be better off loving
23   **Wherein:** in which
23   **pregnant enemy:** [the Devil]
24   **proper false:** attractive but deceitful men
25   **set their forms:** make their impression
28   **fadge:** turn out
29   **monster:** unnatural creature [because of her disguise]
30   **dote on:** be infatuated with
31   **As I am man:** while I'm disguised as a man
34   **thriftless:** wasted

Sir Andrew, Sir Toby, and Feste, while Feste sings.
What do the costumes and appearance of Sir Toby and Sir Andrew suggest about what they were doing before they arrived? Shakespeare wrote the part of Feste as a man. In this production Feste was played by a woman as a woman. What difference do you think this makes?

Music

Twelfth Night is the only Shakespeare play to start and end with music, and music is important throughout the play. Music was an important part of many plays at the time, and became increasingly popular. From about 1600, with the gifted singer and musician Robin Armin in his company, Shakespeare increased the number and complexity of songs in his plays. *Twelfth Night* has a range of songs, from sad ballads to popular 'round' songs (like *Hold thy peace*) that everyone knew and sang.

1 Look at the words of Feste's song. How does this song underline the theme of love in the play?

Act 2 Scene 3

Enter Sir Toby and Sir Andrew.

Sir Toby	Approach, Sir Andrew. Does not our lives consist of the four elements?
Sir Andrew	Faith, so they say, but I think it rather consists of eating and drinking.
Sir Toby	Th' art a scholar; let us therefore eat and drink.　　5 *[Shouting to someone not in the room.]* Maria, I say, a stoup of wine!

Enter Feste.

Sir Andrew	Here comes the Fool, i' faith.
Feste	How now, my hearts?
Sir Toby	Welcome, ass.　　10
Sir Andrew	Now a song.
Sir Toby	*[Giving Feste money.]* Come on, there is sixpence for you. Let's have a song.
Feste	Would you have a love song, or a song of good life?
Sir Toby	A love song, a love song.　　15
Sir Andrew	Ay, ay. I care not for good life.
Feste	*[Sings.] What is love? 'Tis not hereafter.* *Present mirth hath present laughter.* *What's to come is still unsure.* *In delay there lies no plenty,*　　20 *Then come kiss me, sweet and twenty.* *Youth's a stuff will not endure.*
Sir Andrew	A mellifluous voice, as I am true knight.
Sir Toby	A contagious breath.
Sir Andrew	Very sweet and contagious, i' faith.　　25
Sir Toby	But shall we make the welkin dance indeed? Shall we do that?
Sir Andrew	An you love me, let's do't. I am dog at a catch.
Feste	By'r Lady sir, and some dogs will catch well.
Sir Andrew	Most certain. Let our catch be "Thou Knave".　　30
Feste	"Hold thy peace, thou knave", knight?
Sir Andrew	Begin, Fool. It begins "Hold thy peace".
Feste	I shall never begin if I hold my peace.
Sir Andrew	Good i' faith. Come, begin.

Feste starts singing, then each one joins in when the previous person has finished the first line. The song gets very loud.

Enter Maria.

2　the four elements: it was thought everything was made up of: earth, air fire and water

9　my hearts: my good friends

10　ass: [i.e. Feste. The fool, is an idiot]

17　hereafter: to put off for the future

20　plenty: profit

22　Youth's a stuff … endure: you won't be young forever

23　mellifluous: sweet as honey

24　contagious breath: double meaning: 1) infectious breath; 2) catchy song; Sir Toby puns on this

26　welkin: sky

28　a dog at: excellent at

29　By'r Lady: by our Lady [the Virgin Mary], a mild oath

34　Good i' faith: very funny

Malvolio in the modern-dress production (left) and the original-dress production (right).

Does the different costume choice make any difference to how you see Malvolio at this point?

2 In Shakespeare's time the puritans wanted to shut theatres for encouraging bad behaviour. The word 'puritan' (line 61) was used as an insult. How would describing Malvolio as a puritan affect the audience's view of him?

Gulling

In Shakespeare's time someone who was tricked or 'conned' was often said to be 'gulled'. The person tricked was a 'gull' and carrying out the trick was called 'gulling'. All these words are related to the word 'gullible' that is used in modern English. In plays and pamphlets of the time, gulling was often used to trick people out of money. These gulls were seldom innocent – the tricks played on their greed. Either they were asked to join in gulling another person (who was actually part of the con) or they were trying to get something for nothing at the expense of others.

When Maria says she is going to gull Malvolio, Sir Toby and Sir Andrew know she is going to trick on him and so do the audience. They all suspect, even before she tells them, that it is his sense of his own importance that will be used to work the trick. Malvolio, the gull, has no idea he is being tricked.

Maria	What a caterwauling do you keep here! If my lady have not called up her steward Malvolio and bid him turn you out of doors, never trust me.	35
	Enter Malvolio.
Malvolio	My masters are you mad? Or what are you? Have you no wit, manners, nor honesty, but to gabble like tinkers at this time of night? Do ye make an ale-house of my lady's house? Is there no respect of place, persons, nor time in you?	40
Sir Toby	We did keep time, sir, in our catches. Sneck up!
Malvolio	Sir Toby, I must be round with you. My lady bade me tell you, that, if you can separate yourself and your misdemeanours, you are welcome to the house. If not, she is very willing to bid you farewell.	45
Sir Toby	*[Singing.] Farewell, dear heart, since I must needs be gone.*
Maria	Nay, good Sir Toby.	50
Sir Toby	Art any more than a steward? — A stoup of wine, Maria!
Malvolio	Mistress Mary, if you prized my lady's favour at anything more than contempt, you would not give means for this uncivil rule. She shall know of it, by this hand. *He exits.*	55
Maria	Go shake your ears! Sweet Sir Toby, for Monsieur Malvolio, let me alone with him. If I do not gull him and make him a common recreation, do not think I have wit enough to lie straight in my bed.
Sir Toby	Possess us, possess us, tell us something of him.	60
Maria	The devil a puritan that he is, a time-pleaser; an affectioned ass, so crammed (as he thinks) with excellencies, that it is his grounds of faith that all that look on him, love him. And on that vice in him will my revenge find notable cause to work.	65
Sir Toby	What wilt thou do?
Maria	I will drop in his way some obscure epistles of love. I can write very like my lady your niece. We can hardly make distinction of our hands.
Sir Toby	Excellent, I smell a device.	70
Sir Andrew	I have't in my nose too.
Sir Toby	He shall think by the letters that thou wilt drop that they come from my niece, and that she's in love with him.
Maria	My purpose is indeed a horse of that colour.
Sir Andrew	And your horse now would make him an ass.	75
Maria	Ass, I doubt not.

---

35 caterwauling: awful noise

39 honesty: respect
39 tinkers: travelling mender of pots, pans and other household items

43 Sneck up!: Shut up!
44 round: blunt
44 bade: instructed

50 Art: are you

52–4 prized … uncivil rule: valued my lady's good opinion you would not encourage this behaviour
54–5 by this hand: I swear

57 let me … him: leave him to me
57 gull: trick

60 Possess us: tell us
61 puritan: strict, over-moral
61 The devil …is: He's not a genuine puritan
61 time-pleaser: flatterer
62 affectioned: affected, pretentious
63 it is … of faith: he truly believes
65 notable cause to work: enough ammunition
67 obscure epistles: ambiguous letters
69 hands: handwriting
70 a device: a trick

74 a horse of that colour: that

Sir Andrew.
Does this photograph
show a different side of
Sir Andrew's character
than we have seen so far?

Sir Andrew	O, 'twill be admirable!	
Maria	Sport royal, I warrant you. For this night, to bed, and dream on the event. Farewell. *She exits.*	
Sir Andrew	Before me, she's a good wench.	80
Sir Toby	She's a beagle true bred, and one that adores me. What o' that?	
Sir Andrew	I was adored once too.	
Sir Toby	Let's to bed knight. Thou hadst need send for more money.	85
Sir Andrew	If I cannot recover your niece, I am a foul way out.	
Sir Toby	Come, come, I'll go burn some sack. 'Tis too late to go to bed now. Come knight, come knight.	
	They exit.	

80 Before me: a mild oath

81 beagle: skilful hunting dog

84 Thou hadst need: you had better

86 recover: win [i.e. marry]

86 I am ... way out: I'll have spent a fortune for nothing

87 burn some sack: warm some wine

Act 2 Scene 4

Enter Orsino, Cesario (Viola disguised as a man), and Curio.

Orsino	Give me some music.	
Curio	He is not here, so please your lordship, that should sing it.	
Orsino	Who was it?	
Curio	Feste the jester my lord, a fool that the Lady Olivia's father took much delight in. He is about the house.	5
Orsino	Seek him out *Curio exits.* [*To Viola.*] Come hither, boy. If ever thou shalt love, In the sweet pangs of it, remember me. For such as I am, all true lovers are, Unstaid and skittish in all motions else Save in the constant image of the creature That is beloved. How dost thou like this tune?	10
Cesario (Viola)	It gives a very echo to the seat Where love is throned.	
Orsino	Thou dost speak masterly. My life upon't, young though thou art, thine eye Hath stayed upon some favour that it loves. Hath it not boy?	15
Cesario (Viola)	A little, by your favour.	
Orsino	What kind of woman is't?	
Cesario (Viola)	Of your complexion.	
Orsino	She is not worth thee then. What years, i' faith?	20
Cesario (Viola)	About your years, my lord.	
Orsino	Too old, by heaven. Let still the woman take An elder than herself: so wears she to him,	

What's just happened

- Viola (as Cesario) has tried to woo Olivia for Orsino.
- Olivia has refused Orsino and tried to give Cesario a ring.
- Viola has realised Olivia loves her in her disguise as Cesario.
- Orsino knows nothing about the disguise or the ring.

8 hither: here

11 Unstaid: unrestrained

11 skittish: changeable

11 all motions else: all other emotions

12 Save: except

14–5 gives a very ... throned: faithfully reflects the way the heart feels

15 masterly: like an expert

17 stayed upon: gazed long at

17 some favour: a face

18 by your favour: if you please

22 still: always

23 wears she: she adapts

Orsino and Cesario (Viola) while Feste is singing.
They are both lost in the music. What does their body language
suggest is just about to happen? What do you think did happen?

	So sways she level in her husband's heart.	
	Then let thy love be younger than thyself,	25
	Or thy affection cannot hold the bent.	
	For women are as roses, whose fair flower	
	Being once displayed, doth fall that very hour.	
Cesario (Viola)	And so they are. Alas, that they are so,	
	To die even when they to perfection grow.	30

Enter Feste.

Orsino	O fellow come, the song we had last night. —	
	Mark it Cesario. It is silly sooth,	
	And dallies with the innocence of love,	
	Like the old age.	
Feste	Are you ready, sir?	35
Orsino	Ay, prithee sing.	
Feste	*Come away, come away, death,*	
	And in sad cypress let me be laid.	
	Fly away, fly away, breath,	
	I am slain by a fair cruel maid.	40
	My shroud of white, stuck all with yew, O, prepare it!	
	My part of death, no one so true did share it.	
Orsino	*[Giving him money.]* There's for thy pains.	
Feste	No pains, sir, I take pleasure in singing, sir.	
Orsino	I'll pay thy pleasure then.	45
Feste	Truly sir, and pleasure will be paid, one time or another.	
	Now the melancholy god protect thee. Farewell.	

He exits.

Orsino	Once more, Cesario,	
	Get thee to yond same sovereign cruelty.	
	The parts that Fortune hath bestowed upon her,	50
	Tell her I hold as giddily as fortune.	
	But 'tis that miracle and queen of gems	
	That nature pranks her in, attracts my soul.	
Cesario (Viola)	But if she cannot love you, sir —	
Orsino	I cannot be so answered.	
Cesario (Viola)	Sooth, but you must.	55
	Say that some lady, as perhaps there is,	
	Hath for your love as great a pang of heart	
	As you have for Olivia. You cannot love her.	
	You tell her so. Must she not then be answered?	
Orsino	There is no woman's sides	60
	Can bide the beating of so strong a passion	
	As love doth give my heart. No woman's heart	
	So big, to hold so much. They lack retention.	

24 sways she level: she lives in balance with
26 hold the bent: keep steady

32 Mark: take notice of
32 silly sooth: simple truth
33 dallies: plays
34 old age: good old days

36 prithee: I pray thee

37 away: here
38 sad cypress: a cypress-wood coffin

41 yew: symbol of mourning

46 paid: paid for

49 yond ... cruelty: [i.e. Olivia]
50 parts: attributes [here: wealth]
51 as giddily: as lightly
51 as Fortune: Fortune was seen as very changeable
52 that miracle ... gems: her beauty
53 pranks: dresses

55 Sooth: in God's truth

57 pang of heart: heartfelt love

59 be answered: accept your answer
61 bide: endure
63 they lack retention: they could not hold it
64 mine: my love

1 What does the speech where Cesario (Viola) talks about the 'worm i' th' bud' add to the atmosphere of this scene?

2 What does the audience learn about Orsino's views of love in this scene?

3 In Shakespeare's time, many people thought men were superior to women. In this scene, Orsino says a man's love is more powerful than a woman's, because 'No woman's heart | So big, to hold so much'. How does Cesario (Viola) try to show Orsino that his view is wrong?

Cesario (Viola) and Orsino.
Was this photograph more likely to have been taken between lines 67–69, or lines 78–81?

But mine is all as hungry as the sea,
And can digest as much. Make no compare   **65**
Between that love a woman can bear me,
And that I owe Olivia.

Cesario (Viola) Ay, but I know —

Orsino   What dost thou know?

Cesario (Viola) Too well what love women to men may owe.
In faith, they are as true of heart as we.   **70**
My father had a daughter loved a man,
As it might be, perhaps, were I a woman,
I should your Lordship.

Orsino   And what's her history?

Cesario (Viola) A blank, my lord. She never told her love,
But let concealment, like a worm i' th' bud   **75**
Feed on her damask cheek. She pined in thought,
And with a green and yellow melancholy
She sat like Patience on a monument,
Smiling at grief. Was not this love indeed?

Orsino But died thy sister of her love, my boy?   **80**

Cesario (Viola) I am all the daughters of my father's house,
And all the brothers too *[Aside.]* and yet I know not.
— Sir, shall I to this lady?

Orsino   Ay, that's the theme.
To her in haste. *[Handing her a jewel.]*
               Give her this jewel. Say
My love can give no place, bide no denay.   **85**

They exit.

Act 2 Scene 5

Enter Sir Toby, Sir Andrew, and Fabian.

Sir Toby Come thy ways, Signior Fabian.

Fabian Nay, I'll come. If I lose a scruple of this sport, let me be
boiled to death with melancholy.

Enter Maria.

Sir Toby Here comes the little villain.

Maria Malvolio's coming down this walk. Observe him for   **5**
the love of mockery, for I know this letter will make a
contemplative idiot of him. Close, in the name of jesting!
The men hide. Maria puts down a letter, then exits.

Enter Malvolio.

Malvolio 'Tis but fortune, all is fortune. Maria once told me she
did affect me, and I have heard herself come thus

---

67 owe: have for

73 history: story

75 a worm i' th' bud: a canker worm eating away a rosebud
76 damask: rose-pink
77 green and yellow: sickly

83 theme: plan, idea
85 can given no place: can't give in
85 bide no denay: don't take no for an answer

1 Come thy ways: come on
2 a scruple: the smallest part

5 walk: path

7 contemplative: moon-struck, staring
7 Close: stay hidden
8 she: [i.e. Olivia]
9 did affect: was fond of
9 thus near: this close to saying so

Malvolio. (Sir Toby, Sir Andrew and Fabian hide in the box tree.) Which line do you think was being spoken when this photograph was taken: 25–6, 36, or 42?

	near, that should she fancy, it should be one of my complexion. Besides, she uses me with a more exalted respect than anyone else that follows her. What should I think on't?	10
Sir Toby	*[Malvolio does not hear any of the things said by Sir Toby, Fabian and Sir Andrew in hiding.]* Here's an overweening rogue.	
Fabian	O peace! Contemplation makes a rare turkey-cock of him. How he jets under his advanced plumes!	15
Sir Andrew	'Slight, I could so beat the rogue!	
Sir Toby	Peace I say.	
Malvolio	To be Count Malvolio.	
Sir Toby	Ah, rogue!	20
Sir Andrew	Pistol him, pistol him!	
Sir Toby	Peace, peace!	
Malvolio	Having been three months married to her, sitting in my state, calling my officers about me, in my branched velvet gown, having come from a daybed, where I have left Olivia sleeping —	25
Sir Toby	Fire and brimstone!	
Fabian	O peace, peace.	
Malvolio	And then to ask for my kinsman Toby —	
Sir Toby	Bolts and shackles!	30
Malvolio	Seven of my people, with an obedient start, make out for him. I frown the while, and perchance wind up my watch, or play with my — some rich jewel. Toby approaches; curtsies there to me —	
Sir Toby	Shall this fellow live?	35
Malvolio	I extend my hand to him thus, quenching my familiar smile with an austere regard of control, saying, "Cousin Toby, my fortunes having cast me on your niece, give me this prerogative of speech —"	
Sir Toby	And does not Toby take you a blow o' the lips then? What, what?	40
Malvolio	"You must amend your drunkenness."	
Sir Toby	Out scab!	
Fabian	Nay, patience.	
Malvolio	"Besides, you waste the treasure of your time with a foolish knight —"	45
Sir Andrew	That's me, I warrant you.	
Malvolio	"One Sir Andrew."	
Sir Andrew	I knew 'twas I, for many do call me fool.	

10 **should she fancy:** if she loved
11 **uses me:** treats me
12 **follows:** serves
14 **overweening:** arrogant
15 **rare:** exceptional
15 **turkey-cock:** male turkey, said to be very vain
16 **jets:** struts
16 **advanced plumes:** raised neck feathers
17 **'Slight:** by God's light, an oath
21 **Pistol:** shoot
24 **my state:** my grand chair
24 **officers:** servants
24 **branched:** embroidered
30 **Bolts and shackles!:** put him in prison chains
34 **curtsies:** bows
36 **familiar:** friendly
37 **austere regard of control:** stern look of a superior person
39 **prerogative:** right
40 **take you … lips:** give you a punch in the mouth
42 **amend:** change

Malvolio, 'M' – why, that begins my name! (lines 73–4).
The actor playing Malvolio was standing at the front of the stage.
Who is he looking at? Why might he have made this choice?

1 If you were directing a performance of the play, how would you tell the actor playing Malvolio to move and speak as he reads the letter?

Malvolio	*[Seeing the letter.]* What employment have we here? 50 *[Picking up the letter.]* By my life, this is my lady's hand. These be her very c's, her u's, and her t's, and thus she makes her great P's. It is in contempt of question her hand.
Sir Andrew	Her c's, her u's, and her t's. Why that? 55
Malvolio	*[Reading.] To the unknown beloved, this, and my good wishes.* Her very phrases! *[Opening the letter.]* 'Tis my lady! To whom should this be?
Fabian	This wins him, liver and all.
Malvolio	*[Reading.] Jove knows I love, but who?* 60 *Lips, do not move, no man must know.* "No man must know." What follows? The numbers altered. "No man must know." If this should be thee, Malvolio!
Sir Toby	Marry, hang thee, brock! 65
Malvolio	*[Reading.] I may command where I adore,* *M.O.A.I. doth sway my life.*
Fabian	A riddle.
Sir Toby	Excellent wench, say I.
Malvolio	"M.O.A.I. doth sway my life." Nay, but first let me see, 70 let me see, let me see. "I may command where I adore." Why, she may command me. I serve her, she is my lady. What should that alphabetical position portend? "M.O.A.I." ... "M." Malvolio. "M" — why, that begins my name! "A" should follow, but "O" does. "M.O.A.I." — 75 every one of these letters are in my name. Soft, here follows prose. *[Reading.] If this fall into thy hand, revolve. In my stars I am above thee, but be not afraid of greatness. Some are born great, some achieve greatness, and* 80 *some have greatness thrust upon 'em. Cast thy humble slough and appear fresh. Be opposite with a kinsman, surly with servants. She thus advises thee that sighs for thee.* *Remember who commended thy yellow stockings,* 85 *and wished to see thee ever cross-gartered. I say, remember. Go to, thou art made if thou desirest to be so. If not, let me see thee a steward still. Farewell. She that would alter services with thee,* *The Fortunate-Unhappy.* 90 Every reason excites to this, that my lady loves me. She did commend my yellow stockings of late, she did praise my leg being cross-gartered, and in this she manifests herself to my love. I thank my stars, I am happy. I will be

50 employment: business [i.e. the letter]

53 in contempt of question: unquestionably

59 liver: thought to control passion

60 Jove: king of the Roman gods

62–3 the numbers altered: the metre has changed

65 brock: badger

67 sway: rule

73 portend: mean

78 revolve: consider this

81–2 cast thy ... appear fresh: throw off your old humble ways

85 commended: praised

86 cross-gartered: with complicated bands holding them up

87 thou art made: your fortune's made

89 alter services: change places (to become a wife obeying her husband, not a Lady giving orders to her servant)

91 excites: leads to

92 of late: recently

93 manifests: shows

94 happy: fortunate in love

Malvolio.
Was this photograph more likely to have been taken between lines 94–5, or lines 99–100?

	strange, stout, in yellow stockings, and cross-gartered, **95** even with the swiftness of putting on. Here is yet a postscript.
	[Reading.] If thou entertain'st my love, let it appear in thy smiling, thy smiles become thee well. Therefore in thy presence still smile, dear my sweet, I prithee. **100** Jove, I thank thee! I will smile, I will do everything that thou wilt have me. *He exits.*

98 entertain'st: welcome

100 still: always

Sir Toby	I could marry this wench for this device.
Sir Andrew	So could I too.

Enter Maria.

Fabian	Here comes my noble gull-catcher. **105**
Maria	Does it work upon him?
Sir Toby	Like aqua vitae with a midwife.
Maria	If you will then see the fruits of the sport, mark his first approach before my lady. He will come to her in yellow stockings, and 'tis a colour she abhors, and **110** cross-gartered, a fashion she detests. And he will smile upon her, which will now be so unsuitable to her disposition, being addicted to a melancholy as she is, that it cannot but turn him into a notable contempt. If you will see it, follow me. **115**
Sir Toby	Thou most excellent devil of wit!
Sir Andrew	I'll make one, too. *They exit.*

105 gull-catcher: con artist

107 aqua vitae: brandy

108 fruits: outcome

110 abhors: loathes

114 turn him … contempt: make her contemptuous of him

117 make one: come along

These questions are about all of Act 2 Scene 5.

2 At the time the play was written, the rigid organisation of society meant that a servant such as Malvolio could not normally marry into the nobility. How would an audience in Shakespeare's time feel about Malvolio's idea that he could become Olivia's husband, even though she is a countess?

3 How do Malvolio's words and actions in this scene develop the themes of pride and ambition?

4 What aspects of Malvolio's character help to make Maria's trick such a success?

These questions ask you to reflect on all of Act 2.

a) How does Malvolio's language in Act 2 show his pride and self-importance?

b) How does Malvolio's behaviour contrast with the way Sir Toby and the others behave in Act 2?

c) How is the battle between serious behaviour and enjoying life developed in the events in Act 2?

d) In thinking about the events in Act 2, how important do you feel it is to understand society's rigid organisation in Shakespeare's time?

e) How are the characters of Orsino and Olivia shown to be quite similar in Act 2?

A

What's just happened

- Orsino has sent Cesario (Viola) back to woo Olivia for him.
- Sir Andrew wants Olivia to take him seriously as a suitor.
- Olivia, in love with Cesario, sent a ring after him, pretending she was returning a gift from Orsino.

What will Cesario (Viola) be feeling?

Feste and Cesario (Viola).
These photographs were taken between lines 1 and 21. They are not in the order they were taken in. (i.e. A was not the first one taken). What is the right order?

1 How have the director and the designer made it clear who is the gentleman and who is the Fool?

2 How is this reflected in the way they speak to each other?

B

C

46

Act 3 Scene 1

Enter Cesario (Viola disguised as a man) and Feste, playing a tabor.

Cesario (Viola)	Save thee, friend. Dost thou live by thy tabor?
Feste	No, sir, I live by the church.
Cesario (Viola)	Art thou a churchman?
Feste	No such matter sir. I do live by the church. For I do live at my house, and my house doth stand by the church. 5
Cesario (Viola)	Art not thou the Lady Olivia's Fool?
Feste	No indeed sir. She will keep no fool, sir, till she be married. I am indeed not her Fool, but her corrupter of words.
Cesario (Viola)	I saw thee late at the Count Orsino's. 10
Feste	Foolery, sir, does walk about the orb like the sun, it shines everywhere.
Cesario (Viola)	I'll no more with thee. Hold, *[Giving a coin.]* there's expenses for thee.
Feste	Now Jove, in his next commodity of hair, send thee a 15 beard.
Cesario (Viola)	By my troth I'll tell thee, I am almost sick for one, *[Aside.]* though I would not have it grow on my chin. *[To Feste.]* Is thy lady within?
Feste	My lady is within, sir. I will conster to them whence 20 you come. *He exits.*
Cesario (Viola)	This fellow is wise enough to play the fool, And to do that well, craves a kind of wit.

Enter Sir Toby and Andrew.

Sir Toby	Save you, gentleman.
Cesario (Viola)	And you sir. 25
Sir Andrew	*Dieu vous garde, monsieur.*
Cesario (Viola)	*Et vous aussi, votre serviteur!*
Sir Andrew	I hope sir, you are, and I am yours.
Sir Toby	Will you encounter the house? My niece is desirous you should enter, if your trade be to her. 30
Cesario (Viola)	I am bound to your niece, sir.

Enter Olivia, and Maria.

	Most excellent accomplished lady, the heavens rain odours on you.
Sir Andrew	*[Aside.]* That youth's a rare courtier. "Rain odours," well. 35

---

1 Save thee: 'God save thee', a greeting

1 live by: double meaning: 1) make a living from; 2) live next to

1 tabor: drum

10 late: recently

11 the orb: the Earth

13 Hold: wait

14 expenses: money

15 commodity: handing out

20 conster: explain

20 them: Olivia's servants

20 whence: from where

23 craves: requires

26 *Dieu ... garde:* 'God save you' in French

27 *Et vous ... serviteur:* 'And you, sir, your servant' in French

31 bound to: coming to see

32 the heavens: may the heavens

33 odours: sweet smells

34 rare: exceptionally good

35 well: that's well put

Olivia and Cesario (Viola).
How do the actors show Olivia's love for Cesario? How do the actors show Viola's reaction?

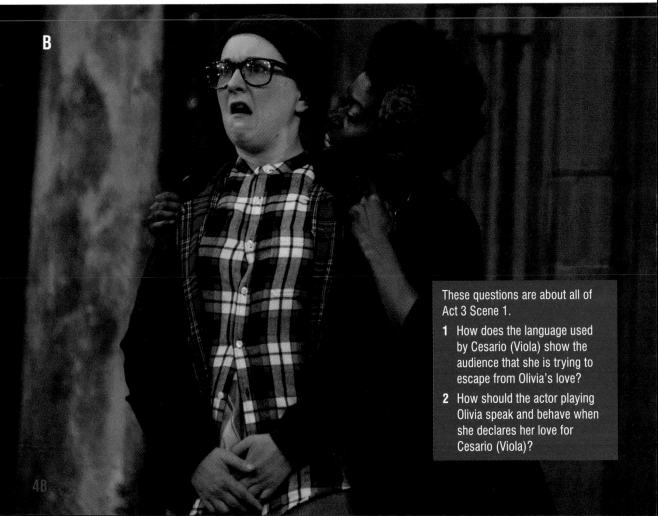

These questions are about all of Act 3 Scene 1.

1 How does the language used by Cesario (Viola) show the audience that she is trying to escape from Olivia's love?

2 How should the actor playing Olivia speak and behave when she declares her love for Cesario (Viola)?

Olivia	Let the garden door be shut, and leave me to my hearing. *Maria, Sir Toby, Sir Andrew exit.* Give me your hand sir.
Cesario (Viola)	My duty, madam, and most humble service.
Olivia	What is your name? 40
Cesario (Viola)	Cesario is your servant's name, fair princess.
Olivia	My servant, sir? Y'are servant to the Count Orsino, youth.
Cesario (Viola)	And he is yours, and his must needs be yours. Your servant's servant is your servant, madam. 45
Olivia	For him, I think not on him. For his thoughts, Would they were blanks rather than filled with me.
Cesario (Viola)	Madam, I come to whet your gentle thoughts On his behalf.
Olivia	O by your leave, I pray you. I bade you never speak again of him. 50 But would you undertake another suit, I had rather hear you to solicit that Than music from the spheres.
Cesario (Viola)	Dear lady —
Olivia	Give me leave, I beseech you. I did send, After the last enchantment you did here, 55 A ring in chase of you. So did I abuse Myself, my servant and, I fear me, you. To force that on you in a shameful cunning Which you knew none of yours. What might you think? Let me hear you speak. 60
Cesario (Viola)	I pity you.
Olivia	That's a degree to love.
Cesario (Viola)	No, for 'tis a vulgar proof That very oft we pity enemies.
Olivia	Why then methinks 'tis time to smile again. O world, how apt the poor are to be proud! 65 *A clock strikes.* The clock upbraids me with the waste of time. Be not afraid, good youth, I will not have you. And yet when wit and youth is come to harvest, Your wife is like to reap a proper man. There lies your way, due west.
Cesario (Viola)	Then westward ho! 70 Grace and good disposition attend your Ladyship.
Olivia	Stay. I prithee tell me what thou think'st of me.
Cesario (Viola)	That you do think you are not what you are.

37 **hearing:** private conversation

44 **must needs be:** has to be

47 **blanks:** blank sheets of paper
48 **whet:** sharpen

51–3 **would you … spheres:** if only you'd court me yourself that would be music to my ears

54 **Give me … beseech you:** please, let me speak
55 **enchantment:** magic
56 **in chase of you:** after you
56 **abuse:** do wrong to
57 **I fear me:** I fear
58–9 **To force … of yours:** for having forced on you, by an unworthy trick, a ring you did not bring

61 **a degree to:** a step towards

62 **vulgar proof:** common saying

64 **methinks:** it seems to me
65 **apt:** inclined

66 **upbraids:** reproaches
67 **I will not have you:** I can't force you to marry me
68 **wit and … harvest:** when you're older
69 **reap:** gather in [the harvest]
69 **proper:** respectable
71 **disposition:** frame of mind

Sir Andrew and Sir Toby.
Why has the director chosen to give Sir Andrew a suitcase as a prop?

These questions are about the whole of Act 3 Scene 2.

1 How do Sir Toby's words show that he is not treating Sir Andrew as a true friend?

2 How do Sir Toby's actions in this scene change the way the audience feels about him?

Olivia	If I think so, I think the same of you.	
Cesario (Viola)	Then think you right: I am not what I am.	**75**
Olivia	Cesario, by the roses of the spring,	
	By maidhood, honour, truth, and everything,	
	I love thee. So that maugre all thy pride,	
	Nor wit nor reason can my passion hide.	
	Do not extort thy reasons from this clause,	**80**
	For that I woo, thou therefore hast no cause.	
	But rather reason thus with reason fetter;	
	Love sought is good, but given unsought is better.	
Cesario (Viola)	By innocence I swear, and by my youth,	
	I have one heart, one bosom, and one truth,	**85**
	And that no woman has, nor never none	
	Shall mistress be of it, save I alone.	
	And so adieu, good madam, never more	
	Will I my master's tears to you deplore.	
Olivia	Yet come again, for thou perhaps mayst move	**90**
	That heart which now abhors, to like his love.	

They exit at different doors.

Act 3 Scene 2

Enter Sir Toby, Sir Andrew, and Fabian.

Sir Andrew	No, faith, I'll not stay a jot longer.
Sir Toby	Thy reason, dear venom, give thy reason.
Sir Andrew	Marry, I saw your niece do more favours to the Count's servingman than ever she bestowed upon me. I saw't i' th' orchard.
Sir Toby	Did she see thee the while, old boy? Tell me that.
Sir Andrew	As plain as I see you now.
Fabian	This was a great argument of love in her toward you.
Sir Andrew	'Slight! will you make an ass o' me?
Fabian	She did show favour to the youth in your sight only to exasperate you, to awake your dormouse valour. You should then have accosted her, and with some excellent jests, you should have banged the youth into dumbness.
Sir Toby	Challenge me the Count's youth to fight with him. Hurt him in eleven places, my niece shall take note of it, and assure thyself, there is no love-broker in the world can more prevail in man's commendation with woman than report of valour.

77 maidhood: virginity
78 maugre: in spite of
79 Nor … nor: neither … nor
80 extort … clause: don't reason from this
81 For that: because
81 no cause: no need to woo
82 with reason fetter: chaining up you reasoning
86 nor never none: nor any, ever
87 save: except
89 deplore: describe, weeping

1 jot: moment
2 venom: angry one
4 bestowed upon: gave
6 the while: at the time
8 argument: proof
9 'Slight: by God's light, an oath
11 dormouse: sleepy
12 accosted: several meanings: approached, greeted, wooed
13–14 banged … dumbness: struck the youth dumb
15 Challenge … with him: challenge the Count's young man to a duel
17 love-broker: matchmaker
18 commendation: approval

These questions are about all of Act 3 Scene 3.

1 How do the words Antonio uses in this scene show that it is dangerous for him to be in the city ruled by Orsino?

2 What do Antonio's actions in this scene tell an audience about his character?

Fabian	There is no way but this, Sir Andrew.	20
Sir Andrew	Will either of you bear me a challenge to him?	
Sir Toby	Go, write it, go about it.	

Exit Sir Andrew.

Fabian	This is a dear manikin to you, Sir Toby.
Sir Toby	I have been dear to him, lad, some two thousand strong or so.	25
Fabian	We shall have a rare letter from him.
Sir Toby	By all means stir on the youth to an answer. I think oxen and wainropes cannot hale them together.

Enter Maria.

Maria	If you will laugh yourselves into stitches, follow me. Yond gull Malvolio is in yellow stockings!	30
Sir Toby	And cross-gartered?	
Maria	Most villainously. He does obey every point of the letter that I dropped to betray him. You have not seen such a thing as 'tis. I know my lady will strike him. If she do, he'll smile and take't for a great favour.	35
Sir Toby	Come, bring us, bring us where he is.	

They all exit.

Act 3 Scene 3

Enter Sebastian and Antonio.

Sebastian	My kind Antonio, what's to do? Shall we go see the relics of this town?	
Antonio	Tomorrow, sir. Best first go see your lodging.	
Sebastian	I am not weary, and 'tis long to night. I pray you let us satisfy our eyes With the memorials and the things of fame That do renown this city.	5
Antonio	Would you pardon me. I do not without danger walk these streets. Once, in a sea fight 'gainst the Count his galleys I did some service, of such note indeed That were I ta'en here it would scarce be answered.	10
Sebastian	Belike you slew great number of his people?	
Antonio	Th'offence is not of such a bloody nature, Albeit the quality of the time and quarrel Might well have given us bloody argument.	15

21 bear me: carry for me

23 dear manikin: sweet little puppet

24 dear: expensive

30 gull: dupe, gullible fool

What's just happened

- Antonio has gone with Sebastian to Orsino's city.
- Antonio is has a wanted man there.

Does Sebastian worry about this?

2 relics: famous sights

4 to: until

7 renown: make famous

9 the Count his galleys: the Count [Orsino's] ships

10–1 I did … answered: I did so well that if I'm caught, I'm in trouble

12 Belike: presumably

14 Albeit: even though

14 quality … quarrel: circumstances of the dispute

15 bloody argument: cause for bloodshed

Malvolio, in his yellow stockings.
Compare Malvolio in his yellow stockings from the two productions (this page and page 56). What difference does doing the production in modern dress make?

| | For which if I be lapsèd in this place
I shall pay dear. | **16 lapsèd:** caught |

Sebastian   Do not then walk too open.

Antonio It doth not fit me. Hold, sir, here's my purse.
In the south suburbs at the Elephant
Is best to lodge. I will bespeak our diet   20
Whiles you beguile the time, and feed your knowledge
With viewing of the town. There shall you have me.

Sebastian Why I your purse?

Antonio Your store, I think, is not for idle markets, sir.

Sebastian I'll be your purse-bearer, and leave you   25
For an hour.

Antonio To th' Elephant.

Sebastian I do remember.   *They exit.*

20 bespeak our diet: order our food
21 beguile the time: sightsee
22 have me: find me

24 your store … markets: you don't have money for inessentials

Act 3 Scene 4

Enter Olivia.

Olivia I have sent after him, he says he'll come.
How shall I feast him? What bestow of him?
For youth is bought more oft than begged or borrowed.
                    Maria enters.
I speak too loud.
Where's Malvolio? He is sad, and civil,   5
And suits well for a servant with my fortunes.
[To Maria.] Where is Malvolio?

Maria He's coming madam. But in very strange manner. He is sure possessed, madam.

Olivia Why, what's the matter? Does he rave?   10

Maria No, madam, he does nothing but smile. Your Ladyship were best to have some guard about you if he come, for sure the man is tainted in's wits.

Olivia Go call him hither.   *Exit Maria.*
        I am as mad as he,
If sad and merry madness equal be.   15
    *Enter Malvolio, cross-gartered, in yellow
        stockings, followed by Maria.*
How now, Malvolio?

Malvolio Sweet lady, ho, ho!

Olivia Smil'st thou? I sent for thee upon a sad occasion.

Malvolio Sad, lady? I could be sad. This does make some obstruction in the blood, this cross-gartering, but   20 what of that? If it please the eye of one, it is with me as the very true sonnet is: "Please one, and please all".

What's just happened

- Maria's letter has made Malvolio believe Olivia loves him and wants him to act and dress oddly.
- Olivia knows nothing about the letter or its instructions.

How do you think Malvolio is feeling when Oliva calls for him?

1 him: [i.e. Cesario]
2 feast him: entertain him
2 bestow of: give to
5 sad and civil: serious and polite
6 with my fortunes: in my circumstances
9 sure possessed: certainly mad
10 rave: speak wildly
12 were best to: had better
13 tainted in's: diseased in his
14 hither: here

18 upon a sad occasion: on a serious matter
19–20 some … in the blood: slows the blood's circulation
22 sonnet: here: song

Olivia and Malvolio.
Is this photograph more likely to have been taken when Malvolio was saying line 40, line 42 or line 44?

Olivia	Why, how dost thou, man? What is the matter with thee?	
Malvolio	Not black in my mind, though yellow in my legs.	25
Olivia	Wilt thou go to bed, Malvolio?	
Malvolio	To bed? "Ay, sweetheart, and I'll come to thee".	
Olivia	God comfort thee! Why dost thou smile so and kiss thy hand so oft?	
Maria	How do you, Malvolio?	30
Malvolio	At your request? Yes, nightingales answer daws.	
Maria	Why appear you with this ridiculous boldness before my lady?	
Malvolio	"Be not afraid of greatness." 'Twas well writ.	
Olivia	What mean'st thou by that, Malvolio?	35
Malvolio	"Some are born great —"	
Olivia	Ha?	
Malvolio	"Some achieve greatness —"	
Olivia	What sayst thou?	
Malvolio	"And some have greatness thrust upon them."	40
Olivia	Heaven restore thee!	
Malvolio	"Remember who commended thy yellow stockings —"	
Olivia	Thy yellow stockings?	
Malvolio	"And wished to see thee cross-gartered."	
Olivia	Cross-gartered?	45
Malvolio	"Go to, thou art made, if thou desir'st to be so —"	
Olivia	Am I made?	
Malvolio	"If not, let me see thee a servant still."	
Olivia	Why, this is very midsummer madness.	

Enter Servant.

Servant	Madam, the young gentleman of the Count Orsino's is returned.	50
Olivia	I'll come to him. *Exit Servant.*	
	Good Maria, let this fellow be looked to. Where's my Cousin Toby? Let some of my people have a special care of him.	55

Exit Olivia and Maria through different doors.

Malvolio	O ho, do you come near me now? No worse man than Sir Toby to look to me. This concurs directly with the letter. She sends him on purpose that I may appear stubborn to him, for she incites me to that in the letter: And when she went away now, "Let this fellow be	60

Glossary (right column):

25 **black in my mind:** melancholy

27 **"Ay, sweetheart ... thee":** from a popular song

31 **At your ... answer daws:** I won't answer you: nightingales don't sing back to crows

41 **restore:** cure

49 **midsummer:** said to be the season for madness

53 **looked to:** looked after

56 **come near:** begin to understand
57 **concurs:** agrees

59 **incites:** urges

chose to have Malvolio captured and taken off stage. What effect might this have on the audience?

Madness

In Shakespeare's time many people believed in 'humours'. They thought there were four humours in the body – blood, phlegm, black bile and yellow bile – and that to be healthy, you needed all four to be in balance. Too much black bile was thought to make people mad. People also believed madness could be caused by 'possession' – a devil taking over a person's mind and body. In these cases, the 'mad' person was imprisoned and exorcised (a priest drove out the devil). Olivia believes Malvolio's behaviour is 'midsummer madness' (his humours are out of balance), but the others pretend to think he is possessed, so they put him in a dark prison.

looked to." "Fellow!" Not "Malvolio," nor after my degree, but "fellow." Why, everything adheres together. Nothing that can be, can come between me and the full prospect of my hopes.

Enter Sir Toby, Fabian, and Maria.

Sir Toby	Which way is he, in the name of sanctity?	65
Fabian	Here he is, here he is. *[To Malvolio.]* How is't with you, sir?	
Malvolio	Go off, I discard you. Let me enjoy my private. Go off.	
Maria	Lo, how hollow the fiend speaks within him.	
Sir Toby	*[To Fabian and Maria.]* Go to, go to! Peace, peace, we must deal gently with him. Let me alone. *[To Malvolio.]* How do you, Malvolio? How is't with you? What, man, defy the devil! Consider, he's an enemy to mankind.	70
Malvolio	Do you know what you say?	75
Maria	Pray God he be not bewitched!	
Malvolio	How now, mistress?	
Fabian	No way but gentleness, gently, gently. The fiend is rough, and will not be roughly used.	
Sir Toby	*[To Malvolio.]* Why how dost thou, chuck?	80
Malvolio	Sir!	
Maria	Get him to say his prayers, good Sir Toby, get him to pray.	
Malvolio	My prayers, minx?	
Maria	No, I warrant you, he will not hear of godliness.	85
Malvolio	Go hang yourselves all! You are idle shallow things. I am not of your element. You shall know more hereafter.	

He exits.

Sir Toby	Is't possible?	
Fabian	If this were played upon a stage now, I could condemn it as an improbable fiction.	90
Sir Toby	Come, we'll have him in a dark room and bound. My niece is already in the belief that he's mad.	

Enter Sir Andrew, with a letter.

Sir Andrew	Here's the challenge, read it.	
Sir Toby	Give me. *[Reading.]* *Youth, whatsoever thou art, thou art but a scurvy fellow.*	95
Fabian	Good, and valiant.	
Sir Toby	*[Reading.]* *I will waylay thee going home, where if it be thy chance to kill me thou kill'st me like a rogue and a villain.*	

61 **after my degree:** by my social class

62 **adheres together:** agrees

63 **full prospect:** fulfilment

65 **sanctity:** all that's holy

68 **private:** privacy

69 **Lo:** look
69 **the fiend:** the devil

71 **Let me alone:** let me handle this

80 **chuck:** term of affection

85 **I warrant you:** I swear to you

86–7 **I am not … element:** I'm much too important for you to understand

87 **hereafter:** later

91 **bound:** tied up [mad people were treated this way]

95 **scurvy:** contemptible

A

B

C

Sir Toby and Sir Andrew.
These photographs were taken between lines 97 and 110. They are not in the order they were taken in (i.e. A was not the first one taken). What is the right order?

Duelling

Although it was illegal, duelling was a popular way to resolve quarrels between men in Shakespeare's time. A duel began with a spoken or written challenge to fight, naming the cause and a time and place to fight. The duel followed, fought with a sword or a rapier. All gentlemen were taught sword fighting. The outcome of the duel was not very important: the aim was to prove your honour and defend your reputation by being prepared to fight. Viola, as a girl, was untrained in sword fighting. Disguised as Cesario, a young man, she was expected to fight.

Fabian	Still you keep o' th' windy side of the law. Good.	100
Sir Toby	*[Reading.] Fare thee well. Thy friend, and thy sworn enemy, Andrew Aguecheek* If this letter move him not, his legs cannot. I'll give't him.	
Maria	You may have very fit occasion for't. He is now in some commerce with my lady, and will by and by depart.	105
Sir Toby	Go, Sir Andrew. Scout me for him at the corner of the orchard. Away! *Sir Andrew exits.* Now will not I deliver his letter, for this letter, being so excellently ignorant, will breed no terror in the youth.	

Enter Olivia and Cesario (Viola disguised as a man).

Fabian	Here he comes with your niece.	110
Sir Toby	I will meditate the while upon some horrid message for a challenge.	

Sir Toby, Fabian and Maria exit.

Olivia	I have said too much unto a heart of stone. Here, wear this jewel for me, 'tis my picture. Refuse it not. It hath no tongue to vex you.	115
	And I beseech you come again tomorrow. What shall you ask of me that I'll deny, That honour, saved, may upon asking give?	
Cesario (Viola)	Nothing but this: your true love for my master.	
Olivia	How with mine honour may I give him that Which I have given to you?	120
Cesario (Viola)	I will acquit you.	121
Olivia	Well, come again tomorrow. Fare thee well. A fiend like thee might bear my soul to hell.	

She exits.

Enter Sir Toby and Fabian.

Sir Toby	Gentleman, God save thee.	
Cesario (Viola)	And you sir.	125
Sir Toby	Of what nature the wrongs are thou hast done him, I know not, but thy intercepter attends thee at the orchard end. Thy assailant is quick, skilful, and deadly.	
Cesario (Viola)	You mistake sir I am sure. No man hath any quarrel to me.	130
Sir Toby	You'll find it otherwise, I assure you.	
Cesario (Viola)	I pray you sir, what is he?	
Sir Toby	He is a devil in private brawl. Souls and bodies hath he divorced three.	

Glossary:
- **100 o' th' windy side:** on the right side (not breaking the law)
- **105 commerce:** business
- **105 by and by:** soon
- **106 Scout me:** keep watch for me
- **111 the while:** while waiting
- **111 horrid:** terrifying
- **118 honour, saved:** except my virginity
- **120 mine honour:** any honesty
- **121 acquit:** excuse
- **127 thy intercepter:** the person lying in wait for you
- **127 attends:** waits for
- **130 to:** with

ABOVE Sir Toby stage manages the fight between the reluctant Cesario and Sir Andrew.
How does the staging show the difference between the two fights?
BELOW Sir Toby and Antonio fight.

Cesario (Viola)	I am no fighter. I have heard of some kind of men that 135 put quarrels purposely on others to taste their valour. Belike this is a man of that quirk.
Sir Toby	Sir, no. His indignation derives itself out of a very competent injury, therefore get you on and give him his desire. 140
Cesario (Viola)	This is as uncivil as strange. I beseech you, do me this courteous office, as to know of the knight what my offence to him is.
Sir Toby	I will do so.

Enter Sir Andrew, Sir Toby talks to him privately.

	Why, man, he's a very devil. 145
Sir Andrew	Pox on't, I'll not meddle with him.
Sir Toby	Ay, but he will not now be pacified. Fabian can scarce hold him yonder.
Sir Andrew	Plague on't, an I thought he had been valiant I'd have seen him damned ere I'd have challenged him. Let 150 him let the matter slip, and I'll give him my horse.
Sir Toby	I'll make the motion. Stand here. *[To Cesario.]* There's no remedy sir, he will fight with you for's oath' sake. He protests he will not hurt you.
Cesario (Viola)	*[Aside.]* Pray God defend me! A little thing would 155 make me tell them how much I lack of a man.
Fabian	Give ground if you see him furious.
Sir Toby	*[To Sir Andrew.]* Come, Sir Andrew, there's no remedy. The gentleman will, for his honour's sake, have one bout with you. But he has promised me, as he is a 160 gentleman and a soldier, he will not hurt you. Come on, to't!
Sir Andrew	*[Drawing his sword.]* Pray God he keep his oath.
Cesario (Viola)	*[To Sir Andrew, drawing her sword.]* I do assure you 'tis against my will. 165

Enter Antonio.

Antonio	*[To Sir Andrew, drawing his sword.]* Put up your sword. If this young gentleman Have done offence, I take the fault on me.
Sir Toby	You sir? Why, what are you?
Antonio	One sir, that for his love dares yet do more Than you have heard him brag to you he will. 170
Sir Toby	*[Drawing his sword.]* Nay, if you be an undertaker, I am for you. *[They prepare to fight.]*

Enter Officers.

136 taste: test
137 Belike: perhaps
137 of that quirk: that sort
139 competent: reasonable
142 courteous office: kind favour
142 as to know of: and ask
146 Pox on't: an oath
148 hold him yonder: keep him there
149 an: if
150 ere: before
152 the motion: the offer
154 for's oath' sake: because he swore to do so
157 Give ground: retreat
160 bout: exchange of blows
166 Put up: put away
171 an undertaker: part of this

An Officer arrests Antonio.
What do you think Antonio is feeling?

Fabian	O good Sir Toby, hold. Here come the officers.
Sir Toby	*[To Antonio.]* I'll be with you anon.
Officer	Antonio, I arrest thee at the suit of Count Orsino. 175
Antonio	You do mistake me, sir.
Officer	No, sir, no jot. I know your favour well, Though now you have no sea-cap on your head.
Antonio	*[To Viola.]* This comes with seeking you. Now my necessity 180 Makes me to ask you for my purse? You stand amazed, I must entreat of you some of that money.
Cesario (Viola)	What money, sir? For the fair kindness you have showed me here, I'll lend you something. My having is not much, 185 I'll make division of my present with you. *[Offering money.]* Hold, there's half my coffer.
Antonio	*[Refusing it.]* Will you deny me now? Do not tempt my misery, Lest that it make me so unsound a man 190 As to upbraid you with those kindnesses That I have done for you.
Cesario (Viola)	I know of none, Nor know I you by voice or any feature.
Antonio	O heavens themselves!
Second Officer	Come sir. 195
Antonio	Let me speak a little. This youth that you see here I snatched one half out of the jaws of death, And to his image, did I devotion.
First Officer	What's that to us? Away!
Antonio	But O, how vile an idol proves this god! 200 Thou hast, Sebastian, done good feature shame. In nature there's no blemish but the mind: None can be called deformed but the unkind.
First Officer	Come, come sir.
Antonio	Lead me on. *The Officers lead Antonio off stage.* 205
Cesario (Viola)	*[Aside.]* Methinks his words do from such passion fly That he believes himself. So do not I. Prove true, imagination, O prove true, That I, dear brother, be now ta'en for you. He named Sebastian. O if it prove, 210 Tempests are kind, and salt waves fresh in love! *She exits.*
Sir Toby	A very dishonest paltry boy, in leaving his friend here in necessity, and denying him.
Sir Andrew	'Slid, I'll after him again and beat him.

They exit.

---

173 **hold:** stop

174 **anon:** right away

177 **favour:** face

179 **comes with:** is the result of

181 **amazed:** bewildered

186 **my present:** what I have
187 **coffer:** money
188 **deny:** reject
189 **tempt:** test
190 **unsound:** unworthy
191 **upbraid:** reproach

198 **And to his … devotion:** looked after him devotedly [begins a run of religious imagery]

201 **hast, Sebastian, done … shame:** have shown how hollow your good looks are

209 **ta'en:** mistaken
210 **prove:** is really him
212 **dishonest:** dishonourable
212 **paltry:** worthless
213 **necessity:** desperate need
213 **denying him:** saying he does not know him
214 **'Slid:** mild oath: 'by God's eyelid'

What's just happened

- The twins (Viola and Sebastian) look so alike that Antonio has already mistaken Viola (disguised as Cesario) for Sebastian.
- Sir Toby and Fabian have tricked Sir Andrew into fighting Cesario, who (as Viola) is scared and does not know how to fight.
- Cesario has consistently rejected Olivia's offers of love.

How might Sir Toby react to meeting Cesario again?

Sir Toby, Sebastian, and Olivia.
What is Olivia doing?

1 How do Sebastian's words to Feste, Sir Toby and Sir Andrew make it clear to the audience that he is a man, rather than his sister Viola pretending to be Cesario?

2 What impression does Shakespeare give of Sebastian's character in this scene? Think about the way he responds to the other characters in the scene.

Act 4 Scene 1

Enter Sebastian and Feste.

Feste	Will you make me believe that I am not sent for you?
Sebastian	Go to, go to, thou art a foolish fellow. Let me be clear of thee.
Feste	No, I do not know you, nor I am not sent to you by my lady to bid you come speak with her, nor your name **5** is not Master Cesario, nor this is not my nose neither. Nothing that is so is so.
Sebastian	I prithee, vent thy folly somewhere else. Thou know'st not me.
Feste	Vent my folly! He has heard that word of some great **10** man and now applies it to a fool. Vent my folly? I prithee now, ungird thy strangeness, and tell me what I shall vent to my lady? Shall I vent to her that thou art coming?
Sebastian	I prithee depart from me. *[Giving money.]* There's **15** money for thee. If you tarry longer, I shall give worse payment.
Feste	By my troth, thou hast an open hand.
	Enter Sir Andrew, Sir Toby, and Fabian.
Sir Andrew	*[To Sebastian.]* Now, sir, have I met you again? *[Hitting him.]* There's for you. **20**
Sebastian	*[Hitting him back.]* Why, there's for thee, and there, and there. Are all the people mad?
Feste	This will I tell my lady straight. I would not be in some of your coats for two pence. *He exits.*
Sir Toby	Come on, sir, hold! **25**
Sir Andrew	Nay, let him alone.
Sebastian	*[To Sir Toby.]* Let go thy hand!
Sir Toby	Come, sir, I will not let you go. Come, my young soldier, put up your iron. You are well fleshed. Come on.
Sebastian	*[Breaking free.]* I will be free from thee. What wouldst thou now? **30** If thou dar'st tempt me further, draw thy sword.
Sir Toby	*[Drawing his sword.]* What, what? Nay then, I must have an ounce or two of blood from you.
	Enter Olivia.
Olivia	Hold, Toby! On thy life I charge thee hold!

1 **Will … me:** do you want me to

2–3 **Let me … thee:** Go away

8 **vent thy folly:** play the fool

13 **ungird thy strangeness:** stop pretending you don't know me

16 **tarry:** hang around

16–7 **worse payment:** [i.e. a beating]

18 **open hand:** double meaning: generous with money/blows

23 **straight:** immediately

29 **put up your iron:** draw your sword

29 **well fleshed:** tough

31 **tempt:** test

ABOVE Sebastian and Olivia.
Both directors decided to have Olivia kiss Sebastian in this scene. If you were directing the scene, would you have them kiss? And if you did, would it be before or after Sebastian's aside?
BELOW Sebastian, who has just been kissed.

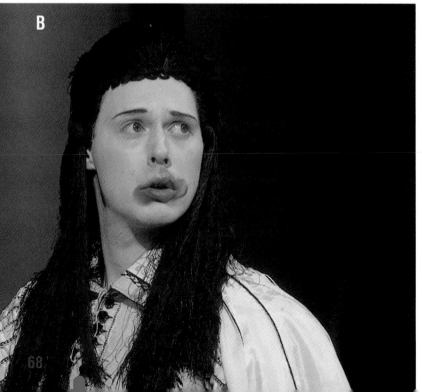

What's just happened

- Malvolio has been tricked into behaving in a mad way in front of Olivia.
- Olivia, shocked by his behaviour, has ordered that he be looked after.
- Instead, Sir Toby, Maria and Feste have locked him in a dark 'prison'.

How different is Malvolio feeling now from when he entered in Act 3 Scene 4 (page 55)?

| Sir Toby | Madam. | 35 |

Olivia	Ungracious wretch, out of my sight!
	— Be not offended, dear Cesario. —
	Rudesby, begone!

Exit Sir Toby, Sir Andrew, and Fabian.

I prithee, gentle friend,
Let thy fair wisdom, not thy passion, sway
In this uncivil and unjust extent   40
Against thy peace. Go with me to my house,
And hear thou there how many fruitless pranks
This ruffian hath botched up, that thou thereby
Mayst smile at this. Thou shalt not choose but go.
Do not deny.   45

Sebastian	*[Aside.]* What relish is in this? How runs the stream?
	Or I am mad, or else this is a dream.
	Let fancy still my sense in Lethe steep;
	If it be thus to dream, still let me sleep.

| Olivia | Nay, come, I prithee. Would thou'dst be ruled by me. | 50 |

| Sebastian | Madam, I will. |

| Olivia | O, say so, and so be! |

They exit.

Act 4 Scene 2

Enter Maria, Sir Toby and Feste.

Maria	Nay, I prithee put on this gown and this beard, make him believe thou art Sir Topas the curate. Do it quickly.
Feste	Well, I'll put it on, and I will dissemble myself in't.
Sir Toby	To him, Sir Topas.
Feste (as Sir Topas)	What ho, I say, peace in this prison.	5
Sir Toby	The knave counterfeits well. A good knave.
Malvolio	*[Within.]* Who calls there?
Feste	Sir Topas the curate, who comes to visit Malvolio the lunatic.
Malvolio	Sir Topas, Sir Topas, good Sir Topas, go to my lady —	10
Feste (as Sir Topas)	Out, hyperbolical fiend, how vexest thou this man! Talkest thou nothing but of ladies?
Malvolio	Sir Topas, never was man thus wronged. Good Sir Topas, do not think I am mad. They have laid me here in hideous darkness.	15

39 Rudesby: ruffian
40–1 uncivil … thy peace: uncalled-for violent assault on you
43 botched up: cobbled together
46 relish: meaning
47 Or: either
48 fancy: imagination
48 in Lethe steep: soak it in the river of forgetfulness
49 still: always

2 curate: priest
3 dissemble: disguise
4 To him: [i.e. Malvolio]
6 counterfeits: plays the part
7 within: [as a stage direction] coming from 'off stage' in the tiring house behind the stage
11 hyperbolical: raging
11 vexest: you torment

Malvolio in his prison.
How might this scene change the
audience's reaction to Malvolio?

Feste	Fie, thou dishonest Satan! Sayst thou that house is dark?
Malvolio	As hell, Sir Topas.
Feste	Madman, thou errest. I say there is no darkness but ignorance.
Malvolio	I say there was never man thus abused. I am no more 20 mad than you are.
Feste	Fare thee well. Remain thou still in darkness..
Sir Toby	My most exquisite Sir Topas.
Maria	Thou mightst have done this without thy beard and gown. He sees thee not. 25
Sir Toby	To him in thine own voice, and bring me word how thou find'st him. I would we were well rid of this knavery, for I am now so far in offence with my niece that I cannot pursue with any safety this sport the upshot. Come by and by to my chamber. 30

Exit Sir Toby and Maria.

Feste	*[Singing, in his own voice.]*
	    Hey, Robin, jolly Robin,
	    Tell me how thy lady does.

Malvolio	Fool!
Feste	*[Singing.]* *My lady is unkind, pardie.*
Malvolio	Fool! 35
Feste	*[Singing.]* *Alas, why is she so?*
Malvolio	Fool, I say!
Feste	*[Singing.]* *She loves another* — Who calls, ha?
Malvolio	Good Fool, help me to a candle, and pen, ink, and paper. As I am a gentleman, I will live to be thankful 40 to thee for't.
Feste	Master Malvolio?
Malvolio	Fool, there was never man so notoriously abused. I am as well in my wits, Fool, as thou art.
Feste	Then you are mad indeed, if you be no better in your 45 wits than a fool.
Malvolio	They keep me in darkness, send ministers to me, asses, and do all they can to face me out of my wits.
Feste	Advise you what you say. The minister is here. *[As Sir Topas.]* Malvolio, Malvolio, thy wits the 50 heavens restore. Endeavour thyself to sleep, and leave thy vain bibble-babble.
Malvolio	Sir Topas!

---

16 that house: that the house

19 thou errest: you're wrong

27 To him: go to him
29 so far in offence: in such deep trouble
30 this … upshot: this trick to the finish

31 by and by: soon

35 *pardie*: by God [*par Dieu* French]

50 Advise you: be careful

53 bibble-babble: gabbling

Sebastian, during his soliloquy.
Which line in the soliloquy was Sebastian probably speaking when this photograph was taken?

1 What words and imagery does Sebastian use at the start of this scene to show that he can hardly believe what is happening to him?

2 How would you ask the actor playing Sebastian to speak and behave, to show the audience his confusion?

Feste	*[As Sir Topas.]* Maintain no words with him, good fellow. *[As himself.]* Who I sir? Not I sir! God b' wi' you, good Sir Topas. *[As Sir Topas.]* Marry, amen. *[As himself.]* I will sir, I will.	55
Malvolio	Fool! Fool! Fool, I say! Help me to some ink, paper, and light, and convey what I will set down to my lady. It shall advantage thee more than ever the bearing of letter did.	60
Feste	I will help you to't. But tell me true, are you not mad indeed, or do you but counterfeit?	
Malvolio	Believe me, I am not. I tell thee true.	65
Feste	Nay, I'll ne'er believe a madman till I see his brains. I will fetch you light, and paper, and ink.	
Malvolio	Fool, I'll requite it in the highest degree. I prithee be gone.	
Feste	*[Singing.] I am gone, sir, and anon, sir,* *I'll be with you again.* *In a trice, like to the old Vice,* *Your need to sustain.* *He exits.*	70

55 **Maintain no word:** don't talk
56–7 **God b' wi' you:** God be with you [goodbye]

60 **convey:** take
61 **advantage:** make money for

68 **requite:** pay you for

70 **anon:** soon
72 **a trice:** an instant
72 **old Vice:** a slow old fool in old plays

Act 4 Scene 3

Enter Sebastian.

Sebastian	This is the air; that is the glorious sun,
	This pearl she gave me, I do feel't and see't,
	And though 'tis wonder that enwraps me thus,
	Yet 'tis not madness. Where's Antonio then?
	I could not find him at the Elephant. 5
	Yet there he was, and there I found this credit,
	That he did range the town to seek me out.
	His counsel now might do me golden service,
	For though my soul disputes well with my sense
	That this may be some error, but no madness. 10
	Yet doth this accident and flood of fortune
	So far exceed all instance, all discourse,
	That I am ready to distrust mine eyes
	And wrangle with my reason that persuades me
	To any other trust, but that I am mad, 15
	Or else the lady's mad. Yet there's something in't
	That is deceivable.

3 **wonder:** amazement
3 **enwraps:** overwhelms

6 **there he was:** he had been there
6 **credit:** information
7 **range:** search all over
8 **counsel:** advice
9 **disputes well:** agrees
11 **accident:** unexpected event
12 **instance:** previous examples
12 **discourse:** reasoned argument
14 **wrangle:** argue
15 **trust:** belief
15 **but:** except
17 **deceivable:** deceptive

Enter Olivia and a Priest.
What are the similarities and differences between the ways the two productions staged this moment?

Enter Olivia, and a Priest.

Olivia	Blame not this haste of mine. If you mean well,	
	Now go with me and with this holy man	
	Into the chantry by. There before him,	20
	And underneath that consecrated roof,	
	Plight me the full assurance of your faith,	
	That my most jealous and too doubtful soul	
	May live at peace. He shall conceal it	
	Whiles you are willing it shall come to note,	25
	What time we will our celebration keep	
	According to my birth. What do you say?	
Sebastian	I'll follow this good man and go with you,	
	And, having sworn truth, ever will be true.	
Olivia	Then lead the way, good father, and heavens so shine	30
	That they may fairly note this act of mine.	

They exit.

20 chantry: private chapel
21 consecrated: blessed
22 Plight me … thy faith: Make a binding promise to marry me
23 jealous: anxious
25 Whiles: until
25 come to note: be made public
26 What time: when
26 our celebration keep: marry
27 birth: social status
29 ever: always
31 fairly note: bring good fortune to

Betrothal and marriage

In Shakespeare's time, a betrothal was when a man and woman promised to marry each other. It was much more serious than a modern engagement, and many couples behaved as if they were married from the moment of the betrothal. Couples did not have to be betrothed, but many were, especially those from wealthy and important families. Betrothals often took place in church, in front of a priest, families and friends. Breaking a betrothal was seen as very wrong. The marriage ceremony could take place soon after a betrothal, or years later.

These questions are about all of Act 4 Scene 3.

3 How would an audience at the time feel about Olivia's determination to carry out the betrothal ceremony as soon as possible?

4 Olivia uses the words 'jealous' and 'doubtful' as she explains her haste to carry out the betrothal ceremony. What does this explanation add to the theme of love in the play?

5 How do Sebastian's feelings about the ceremony contrast with Olivia's? Think about the words he says at the end, and how they contrast with Olivia's explanation for the hasty ceremony.

These questions ask you to reflect on all of Act 4.

a) How is language used to develop the sense of madness and uncertainty through Act 4?

b) How should Sebastian and Olivia's performances change during Act 4?

c) How important is it to know how society in Shakespeare's time treated those with mental illness, to understand the way Malvolio is treated in Act 4?

d) How is the theme of love developed in Act 4?

e) How does Sebastian respond to all that happens to him during Act 4?

What's just happened

- Sebastian has married Olivia (who thinks she has married Cesario). He has also fought, and wounded, Sir Toby and Sir Andrew (who think they were wounded by Cesario).

- Cesario has been mistaken for Sebastian by Antonio, who feels betrayed because he needs the money he gave Sebastian (which Cesario denies having).

- Malvolio has been tricked, locked up in the dark and taunted.

Antonio, with Orsino in the background (between lines 20 to 35).
List the reasons Antonio gives in this speech for being so angry.

Act 5 Scene 1

Enter Feste and, from another door, Orsino, Cesario (Viola) disguised as a man), Curio, and Lords.

Orsino How dost thou, my good fellow? *[Giving Feste a coin.]* There's gold. If you will let your lady know I am here to speak with her, and bring her along with you, it may awake my bounty further.

Feste Marry, sir, lullaby to your bounty till I come again. 5

He exits.

Enter Antonio and Officers.

Cesario (Viola) Here comes the man, sir, that did rescue me.

Orsino That face of his I do remember well,
Yet when I saw it last, it was besmeared
As black as Vulcan in the smoke of war.

First Officer This is that Antonio 10
That took the *Phoenix* and did the *Tiger* board,
When your young nephew, Titus, lost his leg.

Cesario (Viola) He did me kindness sir, drew on my side,
But in conclusion put strange speech upon me.
I know not what 'twas but distraction. 15

Orsino Notable pirate, thou saltwater thief,
What foolish boldness brought thee to their mercies
Whom thou, in terms so bloody and so dear,
Hast made thine enemies?

Antonio Antonio never yet was thief or pirate, 20
Though I confess, on base and ground enough,
Orsino's enemy. A witchcraft drew me hither.
That most ingrateful boy there by your side,
From the rude sea's enraged and foamy mouth
Did I redeem. A wreck past hope he was. 25
His life I gave him and did thereto add
My love, without retention or restraint,
All his in dedication. For his sake
Did I expose myself (pure for his love)
Into the danger of this adverse town, 30
Drew to defend him when he was beset.
Where, being apprehended, his false cunning
Denied me mine own purse,
Which I had recommended to his use
Not half an hour before.

Cesario (Viola) How can this be? 35

Glossary

4 **bounty:** generosity
5 **Marry:** 'By the Virgin Mary', used at the start of a sentence for emphasis as 'Well' is now
5 **lullaby to your bounty:** sing your generosity to sleep
9 **Vulcan:** Roman god of fire, the gods' blacksmith
13 **drew on my side:** drew his sword to defend me
14 **in conclusion... upon me:** after, spoke to me strangely
15 **but distraction:** if not madness
16 **Notable:** notorious
18 **dear:** severe
21 **base and ground enough:** for good reason
24 **rude:** rough
25 **redeem:** save
27 **retention:** reservation
28 **All ... dedication:** it was all his
29 **pure:** just
30 **adverse:** hostile
31 **beset:** attacked
34 **recommended to his use:** given him to use

ABOVE Antonio, restrained by guards, Orsino and Cesario, Maria.
One photograph was taken between lines 49–52; the other between lines 54–57. Which is which?
BELOW Orsino.

Orsino	When came he to this town?
Antonio	Today, my lord. And for three months before,
	Both day and night did we keep company.

Enter Olivia and Attendants.

Orsino	Here comes the Countess. Now heaven walks on earth.
Olivia	Cesario, you do not keep promise with me.	40
Cesario (Viola)	Madam?
Orsino	Gracious Olivia —
Olivia	What do you say, Cesario? Good my lord —
Cesario (Viola)	My lord would speak, my duty hushes me.
Olivia	If it be aught to the old tune, my lord,	45
	It is as fat and fulsome to mine ear
	As howling after music.
Orsino	Still so cruel?
Olivia	Still so constant, lord.
Orsino	What, to perverseness? You uncivil lady,
	To whose ingrate and unauspicious altars	50
	My soul the faithful'st off'rings have breathed out
	That e'er devotion tendered. What shall I do?
Olivia	Even what it please my lord that shall become him.
Orsino	Why should I not (had I the heart to do it)
	Kill what I love? I know the instrument	55
	That screws me from my true place in your favour,
	But this your minion, whom I know you love,
	And whom, by heaven I swear, I tender dearly,
	Him will I tear out of that cruel eye
	Where he sits crownèd in his master's spite.	60
	Come boy, with me. My thoughts are ripe in mischief.
	I'll sacrifice the lamb that I do love,
	To spite a raven's heart within a dove.

He begins to exit.

Cesario (Viola)	And I, most jocund, apt, and willingly,
	To do you rest, a thousand deaths would die.	65

He starts to follow Orsino.

Olivia	Where goes Cesario?
Cesario (Viola)	After him I love
	More than I love these eyes, more than my life,
	More by all mores than e'er I shall love wife.
	If I do feign, you witnesses above
	Punish my life for tainting of my love.	70
Olivia	Ay me detested, how am I beguiled!

40 keep promise with: keep your promise to

43 Good my lord: [to Cesario]

45 aught: anything
46 fat: overblown, gross
46 fulsome: tedious

50 ingrate: ungrateful
50 unauspicious: unfavourable
52 e'er: ever
52 tendered: offered
53 Even … him: whatever you please
55–6 the instrument …favour: who has won your love from me
57 minion: darling
58 tender dearly: value highly
60 in his master's spite: insulting his master
61 ripe in mischief: set on doing harm

64 jocund: cheerful
64 apt: ready
65 To do you rest: to ease your mind

69 feign: pretend
69 witnesses above: gods
70 tainting of: contaminating
71 beguiled: deceived

Sir Andrew,
Is this photograph more likely to have been
taken when he was saying lines 91–2,
lines 97–8 or lines 100–101?

Cesario (Viola)	Who does beguile you? Who does do you wrong?
Olivia	Hast thou forgot thyself? Is it so long?
	— Call forth the holy father. *An attendant exits.*
Orsino	*[To Cesario.]* Come, away!
Olivia	Whither, my lord? — Cesario, husband, stay. **75**
Orsino	Husband?
Olivia	Ay, husband. Can he that deny?
Orsino	Her husband, sirrah?
Cesario (Viola)	No my lord, not I.
	Enter Priest.
Olivia	O welcome, father.
	Father, I charge thee by thy reverence
	Here to unfold what thou dost know **80**
	Hath newly passed between this youth and me.
Priest	A contract of eternal bond of love,
	Confirmed by mutual joinder of your hands,
	Attested by the holy close of lips,
Orsino	*[To Viola.]*
	O thou dissembling cub! What wilt thou be **85**
	When time hath sowed a grizzle on thy case?
	Farewell, and take her, but direct thy feet
	Where thou and I henceforth may never meet.
Cesario (Viola)	My lord, I do protest —
Olivia	O do not swear!
	Hold little faith, though thou hast too much fear. **90**
	Enter Sir Andrew, bleeding from the head.
Sir Andrew	For the love of God, a surgeon! Send one presently to
	Sir Toby!
Olivia	What's the matter?
Sir Andrew	H'as broke my head across, and has given Sir Toby a
	bloody coxcomb too. **95**
Olivia	Who has done this, Sir Andrew?
Sir Andrew	The Count's gentleman, one Cesario. We took him for a
	coward, but he's the very devil incardinate.
Orsino	My gentleman Cesario?
Sir Andrew	'Od's lifelings here he is! *[To Cesario.]* You broke my **100**
	head for nothing, and that that I did, I was set on to do't
	by Sir Toby.
Cesario (Viola)	Why do you speak to me? I never hurt you.
	You drew your sword upon me without cause,

74 **holy father:** priest

77 **sirrah:** sir [used contemptuously]

80 **unfold:** explain
81 **newly passed:** recently occurred
83 **joinder:** joining
84 **Attested:** sealed
83 **close:** meeting
84 **dissembling:** deceitful

86 **grizzle:** sprinkling of grey hair
86 **case:** body
88 **henceforth:** from now on

90 **hold little faith:** keep some part of your promise

91 **presently:** at once

94 **H'as:** he's
95 **bloody coxcomb:** bleeding head

98 **incardinate:** he means 'incarnate': in the flesh

100 **'Od's lifelings:** 'By God's lives': a mild oath

Sebastian, Olivia, Orsino, Cesario (Viola), with a guard in the background.

This photograph was taken just as Viola/Cesario says:

Of Messaline. Sebastian was my father.

Such a Sebastian was my brother too. (136–7)

What do you think all four characters are thinking at this point?

	But I bespake you fair and hurt you not.	105
	Enter Sir Toby, wounded, helped by Feste.	
Sir Andrew	Here comes Sir Toby. If he had not been in drink, he would have tickled you othergates than he did.	
Orsino	*[To Sir Toby.]* How now, gentleman? How is't with you?	
Sir Toby	That's all one. Has hurt me, and there's th' end on't.	109
Sir Andrew	I'll help you, Sir Toby, because we'll be dressed together.	
Sir Toby	Will you help? An ass-head, and a coxcomb, and a knave, a thin-faced knave, a gull?	
	Exit Sir Toby, Sir Andrew, and Feste.	
	From another door, enter Sebastian.	
Sebastian	I am sorry, madam, I have hurt your kinsman. But, had it been the brother of my blood I must have done no less with wit and safety. You throw a strange regard upon me, and by that I do perceive it hath offended you. Pardon me, sweet one, even for the vows We made each other but so late ago.	115
Orsino	One face, one voice, one habit, and two persons! A natural perspective, that is, and is not!	120
Sebastian	Antonio! O my dear Antonio, How have the hours racked and tortured me Since I have lost thee!	
Antonio	Sebastian are you?	
Sebastian	Fear'st thou that, Antonio?	125
Antonio	How have you made division of yourself? An apple cleft in two is not more twin Than these two creatures. Which is Sebastian?	
Olivia	Most wonderful!	
Sebastian	*[Looking at Viola.]* Do I stand there? I never had a brother, Nor can there be that deity in my nature Of here and everywhere. I had a sister, Whom the blind waves and surges have devoured. Of charity, what kin are you to me? What countryman? What name? What parentage?	130 / 135
Cesario (Viola)	Of Messaline. Sebastian was my father. Such a Sebastian was my brother too. So went he suited to his watery tomb. If spirits can assume both form and suit, You come to fright us.	
Sebastian	A spirit I am indeed, But am in that dimension grossly clad	140

105 bespake you fair: spoke to you kindly

106 in drink: drunk
107 othergates: differently

110 be dressed: have our wounds bandaged
111 coxcomb: fool
112 gull: gullible idiot

113 kinsman: relative
114 it been … blood: he been my brother
115 must: could
115 with … safety: in self-defence
116 You throw … me: you're giving me an odd look
118 even for: if only for
119 but so late ago: just now
120 habit: style of dress
121 A natural … not: an optical illusion
123 racked: stretched on the rack [a torture machine]

125 Fear'st thou: do you doubt it

131 deity: god-like ability

134 Of charity: please tell me

138 suited: dressed
139 form and suit: appearance and clothing
140–2 am indeed … participate: this is my human body

Sebastian and Viola.
What impact do you think Sebastian removing
Viola's glasses would have on the audience?

	Which from the womb I did participate.
	Were you a woman, as the rest goes even,
	I should my tears let fall upon your cheek
	And say, "Thrice welcome, drownèd Viola." 145
Cesario (Viola)	My father had a mole upon his brow.
Sebastian	And so had mine.
Cesario (Viola)	And died that day when Viola from her birth
	Had numbered thirteen years.
Sebastian	O, that record is lively in my soul! 150
	He finishèd indeed his mortal act
	That day that made my sister thirteen years.
Viola	If nothing lets to make us happy both
	But this my masculine usurped attire.
	Do not embrace me till each circumstance 155
	Of place, time, fortune, do cohere and jump
	That I am Viola. Which to confirm
	I'll bring you to a captain in this town,
	(Where lie my maiden weeds) by whose gentle help
	I was preserved to serve this noble count. 160
	All the occurrence of my fortune since
	Hath been between this lady and this lord.
Sebastian	*[To Olivia.]* So comes it, lady, you have been mistook.
	You are betrothed both to a maid and man.
Orsino	*[To Olivia.]* Be not amazed, right noble is his blood. 165
	If this be so, as yet the glass seems true,
	I shall have share in this most happy wrack.
	[To Viola.] Boy, thou hast said to me a thousand times
	Thou never shouldst love woman like to me.
Viola	And all those sayings will I overswear, 170
	And all those swearings keep as true in soul
	As doth that orbèd continent the fire
	That severs day from night.
Orsino	Give me thy hand,
	And let me see thee in thy woman's weeds.
Viola	The Captain that did bring me first on shore 175
	Hath my maid's garments. He upon some action
	Is now in durance at Malvolio's suit.
Olivia	Fetch Malvolio hither.
	And yet, alas, now I remember me,
	They say, poor gentleman, he's much distract. 180
	Enter Feste with a letter, and Fabian.
	A most extracting frenzy of mine own

143 as the rest goes even: but the same in every other way

150 record ... soul: memory is clear
151 mortal act: life
153 lets: hinders
154 usurped masculine attire: male disguise

156 cohere and jump: agree [both]

159 maiden weeds: women's clothes

161 occurrence of my fortune: events of my life

163 mistook: mistaken

166 this: all this
166 the glass ... true: and they certainly look alike
167 happy wrack: lucky shipwreck
169 like to: as much as you love
170 overswear: swear all over again

172–3 As doth ... night: as the sun rises and sets each day

176 action: law case
177 in durance: imprisoned
177 suit: accusation
178 hither: here
179 remember me: remember
180 much distract: mad

181 most extracting: all-consuming

Olivia and Malvolio.
Compare Malvolio with when we first saw him (pages 24 and 28). What has changed?

1 How do Malvolio's words emphasise how badly he has been treated?

	From my remembrance clearly banished his.
	[To Feste.] How does he, sirrah?
Feste	Madam, he has here writ a letter to you.
Olivia	Open 't and read it.
Fabian	*[Reading.] By the Lord, madam, you wrong me, and the world shall know it. Think of me as you please. The madly used Malvolio.*
Olivia	Did he write this?
Feste	Ay, madam.
Orsino	This savours not much of distraction.
Olivia	See him delivered, Fabian. Bring him hither.
	My lord, so please you, these things further thought on,
	To think me as well a sister as a wife,
	One day shall crown th' alliance on't, so please you,
	Here at my house and at my proper cost.
Orsino	Madam, I am most apt t' embrace your offer. *[To Viola.]*
	Your master quits you; and for your service done him,
	Here is my hand. You shall from this time be
	Your master's mistress.
Olivia	A sister! You are she.

Enter Malvolio and Fabian.

Orsino	Is this the madman?
Olivia	Ay, my lord, this same.
	— How now, Malvolio?
Malvolio	Madam, you have done me wrong, notorious wrong.
Olivia	Have I, Malvolio? No.
Malvolio	*[Handing her a paper.]*
	Lady, you have. Pray you peruse that letter.
	You must not now deny it is your hand.
	And tell me in the modesty of honour
	Why you have given me such clear lights of favour:
	Bad me come smiling and cross-gartered to you,
	To put on yellow stockings, and to frown
	Upon Sir Toby and the lighter people.
	And acting this in an obedient hope,
	Why have you suffered me to be imprisoned,
	And made the most notorious geck and gull
	That e'er invention played on? Tell me why?
Olivia	Alas, Malvolio, this is not my writing,
	Though I confess much like the character.
	But out of question, 'tis Maria's hand.

Line numbers and glosses:

- **182 From my … his:** drove his madness from my mind
- **185**
- **190**
- **191 savours … distraction:** doesn't sound mad
- **192 delivered:** released
- **195 One day … alliance o'nt:** we'll marry on the same day
- **196 proper cost:** own expense
- **197 apt to embrace:** ready to accept
- **198 quits you:** frees you from service
- **200 mistress:** wife
- **205 peruse:** examine
- **206 must not:** cannot
- **206 hand:** handwriting
- **207 modesty of honour:** name of decency
- **208 lights:** signs
- **211 lighter people:** servants
- **213 suffered me:** allowed me
- **214 geck and gull:** fool
- **215 That … played on?:** who was ever tricked
- **217 character:** style

Viola and Orsino, after line 245.
What is powerful about the staging of this kiss?

	Prithee be content,
	Thou shalt be both the plaintiff and the judge 220
	Of thine own cause.
Fabian	Good madam, hear me speak,

Prithee be content,
Thou shalt be both the plaintiff and the judge   220
Of thine own cause.

Fabian   Good madam, hear me speak,
Most freely I confess, myself and Toby
Set this device against Malvolio here,
Upon some stubborn and uncourteous parts
We had conceived against him. Maria writ   225
The letter at Sir Toby's great importance,
In recompense whereof, he hath married her.
How with a sportful malice it was followed
May rather pluck on laughter than revenge,

Olivia   *[To Malvolio.]* Alas, poor fool, how have they baffled 230
thee!

Feste   Why, "some are born great, some achieve greatness, and
some have greatness thrown upon them." I was one Sir
Topas, sir, but that's all one. "By the Lord, Fool, I am
not mad." But do you remember, "Madam, why laugh 235
you at such a barren rascal, an you smile not, he's
gagged"? And thus the whirligig of time brings in his
revenges.

Malvolio   I'll be revenged on the whole pack of you!

Exit Malvolio.

Olivia   He hath been most notoriously abused.   240

Orsino   Pursue him and entreat him to a peace. *Exit Fabian.*
Cesario, come,
For so you shall be while you are a man.
But when in other habits you are seen,
Orsino's mistress, and his fancy's queen.   245

They all exit, except Feste.

Feste   *When that I was and a little tiny boy,*
     With hey, ho, the wind and the rain,
   A foolish thing was but a toy,
     For the rain it raineth every day.

But when I came to man's estate,   250
     With hey, ho, the wind and the rain,
   'Gainst knaves and thieves men shut their gate,
     For the rain it raineth every day.

---

219 Prithee be content: please be calm
220 plaintiff: accuser
221 cause: case
223 device: plot

224–5 Upon some … against him: because we thought he was being condescending and rude
226 great importance: urging
228 with a sportful malice: like a wicked game
229 pluck on: bring you to
229 than: rather than
230 baffled: disgraced

237 whirligig: spinning top

240 abused: mistreated

245 fancy's: love's

248 foolish thing … toy: silly trick was seen as unimportant

250 came … estate: became a man

Feste, in traditional clothes for a jester or fool.
Why might Shakespeare have chosen to end the play with this song, rather than when all the other characters exit?

But when I came, alas, to wive,
    With hey, ho, the wind and the rain,   255
By swaggering could I never thrive,
    For the rain it raineth every day.

But when I came unto my beds,
    With hey, ho, the wind and the rain,
With tosspots still had drunken heads,   260
    For the rain it raineth every day.

A great while ago the world begun,
    With hey, ho, the wind and the rain,
But that's all one, our play is done,
    And we'll strive to please you every day.   265

He exits.

254 to wive: to marry

256 swaggering: bullying
257 unto my beds: to bed drunk

258 tosspots: drunks

260 drunken heads: hangovers

These questions are about all of Act 5 Scene 1.

2 How would you ask the actor playing Malvolio to speak and behave in this scene?

3 People in Shakespeare's time treated those with mental disabilities as entertainment. How do you think an audience at the time would react to Malvolio's description of the way he has been treated?

4 How is the theme of love brought to a conclusion in this final scene? Think about Viola's and Sebastian's marriages as well as the way in which Malvolio, Sir Andrew and Antonio are left without the love they desired.

5 Before he realises that Cesario (Viola) is in disguise, Orsino threatens to take violent revenge on him. Sir Toby speaks cruelly to his supposed friend Sir Andrew, and Malvolio threatens revenge on everyone as he leaves. Finally, Feste sings a song about how hard life can be. How do these words from these characters affect the mood at the end of the play?

These questions ask you to reflect on all of Act 5.

a) How is the language of madness and confusion mixed with that of love and happiness in Act 5?

b) How should the actors playing Orsino, Olivia, Viola and Sebastian behave when they hear all the surprises that take place in Act 5?

c) A person's position in society was rarely allowed to change at the time when Shakespeare was writing. How has the order of society been restored by the end of Act 5?

d) Twelfth Night is usually thought of as a comedy, but one with a serious aspect. How is the sense of sadness mixed with the happy events of the marriages in Act 5?

e) Viola does not speak after she and Orsino agree to marry. Why do you think she was not given any more to say at the end of the play?

How to do well in assessment

Most importantly, you should aim to enjoy the Shakespeare play that you are reading, and start to think about why Shakespeare makes the characters act as they do and what the main themes of the story are. You should also begin to consider the language that Shakespeare uses. This is also a great start for studying Shakespeare at GCSE.

There is a series of skills that will help you in any assessment of your understanding of a Shakespeare play. They are:

- Read, understand and respond to the play clearly. Comment on the characters' behaviour and motivations, using evidence from the text.

In other words, you need to show that you know the play and can answer the question that you have been given.

- Analyse the language, form and structure that Shakespeare uses. Show your understanding of Shakespeare's techniques by explaining their effects. Use subject terminology.

Here, you show that you understand how the play has been written by commenting on the words and techniques that Shakespeare uses. You should also demonstrate that you understand and can use appropriate technical language.

- Show understanding of the relationship between the play and the context in which it was written.

You must show that you understand the connections between the text and the time when it was written. This could be cultural events, like celebrating Epiphany (the twelfth night after Christmas) when traditional roles were relaxed and the normal order of things could be reversed – such as women dressing as men. Context also covers social customs of the time – such as men fighting duels to defend their honour – and how these affect the way Shakespeare's characters think and behave.

- Use a range of vocabulary and sentence structures for clarity, purpose and effect, with accurate spelling and punctuation.

This means that your work should be clear, organised and well-written. You are not expected to have perfect spelling, but you should spell key words and characters' names correctly and use correct grammar.

Advice for answering questions

Remember the skills that have just been explained. You will not usually have to show every single skill in every answer that you write. For example, extract questions usually require you to cover the first two skills – commenting on characters' behaviour and looking at how the play has been written. Remember that there is no single perfect answer to any question. Write about how you feel about the characters' actions; it is perfectly acceptable to use phrases such as 'I think…', 'I feel that…' and 'In my opinion…' when answering. The most thoughtful responses often show originality, but remember to support your points with sensible argument and evidence from *Twelfth Night*.

1 **Read Act 1 Scene 5, lines 119–49 (pages 21 and 23.) Look at how Olivia speaks and behaves here. How do you think an audience might respond to this part of the play?**

Considering character

- Think about what Olivia says and how she behaves in this extract. Make a list of words that could describe her behaviour, for example: *sarcastic, abrupt, doubtful.*

- Under each of the aspects you have listed, find a short quotation as evidence of Olivia's behaviour. For example: sarcastic – *'Item, two lips indifferent red.'*

- Now build on your ideas by explaining what an audience might think about Olivia from this behaviour. Use the glossary on the right of each page to help you, but remember that the best answers include your own ideas.

For example:

I think that Olivia is quite sarcastic towards Cesario (Viola.) Cesario suggests that it would be a shame if Olivia did not marry and have children, so Olivia gives him (her) a list of her features, such as *'two lips indifferent red,'* that will do instead. She knows that this isn't what Cesario meant, so she's partly mocking her, but I also think she's flirting.

Considering language and technique

To develop the skill of analysing Shakespeare's language and technique, look back at each quotation you have selected and try to say something about particular word choices and their effect on you. For example:

The adjective *'indifferent'* could suggest that Olivia does not think her lips are that special, so the Duke need not keep sending her messages of love. However, it could also mean that Olivia is *'indifferent'* to the Duke. In other words, she has no feelings for him.

2 **Read Act 3 Scene 4, lines 124–156 (pages 61 and 63.) How does Shakespeare create mood and atmosphere in this extract?**

Considering characters' behaviour

- Make three lists, one each for Cesario (Viola), Sir Toby and Sir Andrew, noting their thoughts and feelings. For example, Viola: *confused, frightened*; Sir Toby: *taunting, amused.* Decide which characters behave similarly to or differently from each other.

- Find evidence from the text to support your ideas.

- Explain your ideas by showing what you think each quotation could reveal about the characters and what kind of mood and atmosphere it creates. Remember, it is up to you to decide what kinds of mood there are. For example:

I think that there is a mood of confusion created, when Cesario says *'This is as uncivil as strange'*, because she doesn't know why Sir Andrew wants to fight her. A mood of fear builds up when she exclaims, *'Pray God defend me!'*, suggesting that she cannot see a way out of the fight. Her concern is the opposite to Sir Toby's attitude, which is one of amusement. He is enjoying pretending to help her, when he reports back that *'There's no remedy'*, but really he is lying about Sir Andrew wanting a fight.

Considering language and technique

Comment on Shakespeare's word choices for Cesario (Viola), Sir Toby and Sir Andrew, and look at how they speak. Think about how these help to create atmosphere. There are adjectives to describe the 'fighters,' but they are false and do not really represent these characters. For example:

Sir Toby uses the adjectives, *'quick, skilful, and deadly'* to describe Sir Andrew. This scares Cesario, and could create sympathy for her from the audience, or amusement at the misunderstanding. Shakespeare does this again when he has Sir Andrew believe that Cesario is *'a very devil.'* The audience knows that this is wrong, which adds to the humour.

Considering context

Consider whether the characters' behaviour or language could be affected by the beliefs and expected behaviour of the time, for example:

Defending your honour was very important in Elizabethan times and this helps us to understand why both Cesario and Sir Andrew believe that the other wishes to fight. The importance of honour emphasises the tension in this scene.

3 How does Shakespeare present different kinds of friendships in *Twelfth Night*?

Considering characters

- List friendships in the play, for example: the Captain and Viola, Sir Toby Belch and Sir Andrew Aguecheek. Continue this list. Find one or two scenes that show each of these relationships. For example: the Duke and Cesario (Act 1 Scene 4, Act 2 Scene 4.) Use these scenes to note down the characteristics that each of these friendships has. For example: the Captain comforts Viola.

- Find evidence from the text to support the characteristics that you've thought of. For example: the Captain reassures Viola that her brother held *'acquaintance with the waves'*, so could have swum to safety.

Considering language and technique

Choose one friendship and think about the language that Shakespeare gives the friends when they speak to and about each other. For example, in Act 1 Scene 3, Sir Toby defends Sir Andrew and uses positive adjectives like *'tall'* and *'Sweet'*, but in Act 3 Scene 2, Sir Toby tells Fabian Sir Andrew can be used for his money. What do you think this language tells us about Sir Toby's attitude towards this relationship?

Considering context

Consider whether the friendships could be affected by beliefs of the time. For example, the Captain seems completely accepting of Viola's idea to find employment and therefore a stronger position in society when disguised as a man. Think about whether any of the other friendships in the play could possibly be influenced by beliefs of the time.

Putting your ideas together

The Duke is quick to trust Cesario. In Act 1 Scene 4, Valentine, notes the *'favours'* the Duke has given him, despite only knowing him for three days. The Duke has *'unclasped...the book even of my secret soul.'* The verb *'unclasped'* suggests that this is an open and honest friendship. This is ironic because the audience knows that Cesario is keeping a big secret from the Duke and is actually a woman. She feels that she must keep her gender a secret, as a woman would not be given a prestigious job in the Duke's palace. This reflected Elizabethan attitudes.

Points to remember

You should:

- answer the question, not spend ages retelling the story
- use short, focused quotations
- explain techniques, not just find them.

Practice questions

1 **Read Act 3 Scene 1, lines 61–91 (pages 49 and 51.) Look at how the characters speak and behave here. How do you think an audience might respond to this part of the play? Refer closely to details from the extract to support your answer.**

Olivia	Be not afraid, good youth, I will not have you.	
	And yet when wit and youth is come to harvest,	
	Your wife is like to reap a proper man.	
	There lies your way, due west.	
Cesario (Viola)	Then westward ho!	70
	Grace and good disposition attend your Ladyship.	
Olivia	Stay. I prithee tell me what thou think'st of me.	
Cesario (Viola)	That you do think you are not what you are.	
Olivia	If I think so, I think the same of you.	
Cesario (Viola)	Then think you right: I am not what I am.	75
Olivia	Cesario, by the roses of the spring,	
	By maidhood, honour, truth, and everything,	
	I love thee. So that maugre all thy pride,	
	Nor wit nor reason can my passion hide.	
	Do not extort thy reasons from this clause,	80
	For that I woo, thou therefore hast no cause.	
	But rather reason thus with reason fetter;	
	Love sought is good, but given unsought is better.	
Cesario (Viola)	By innocence I swear, and by my youth,	
	I have one heart, one bosom, and one truth,	85
	And that no woman has, nor never none	
	Shall mistress be of it, save I alone.	
	And so adieu, good madam, never more	
	Will I my master's tears to you deplore.	
Olivia	Yet come again, for thou perhaps mayst move	90
	That heart which now abhors, to like his love.	

They exit at different doors.

2 **Look at how Shakespeare presents the relationship between Olivia and Malvolio at different points in the play.**

3 **One of the themes of *Twelfth Night* is deception. How is this presented in the play?**

Globe Education Shorter Shakespeare

Series Editors: Paul Shuter, Georghia Ellinas

Contributors: Kevin Dyke, Jennifer Edwards, Jane Sheldon, Jane Shuter, Paul Shuter and, for the original text, Patrick Spottiswoode, Georghia Ellinas, Paul Shuter.

The text of this edition is based on a Globe Education text developed from the cut produced by Bill Buckhurst for the 2016 *Playing Shakespeare with Deutsche Bank* production of *Twelfth Night*.

This book is dedicated to Bill Buckhurst and the cast, crew and creatives of the 2016 Playing Shakespeare with Deutsche Bank production of Twelfth Night, who made this play live for thousands of London school students.

Playing Shakespeare with Deutsche Bank is Globe Education's flagship project for London schools, with 20,000 free tickets given to students for a full-scale Shakespeare production created specifically for young people. **www.playingshakespeare.org**

Photo credits:

All photographs are from the Shakespeare's Globe photo library. Full details of the cast and creatives of the featured productions can be found at www.shakespearesglobe.com/ShorterTwelfthNight

John Tramper, 2002 production: 8, 12
Simon Annand, 2012 production: 16, 32 (right), 34, 36, 40, 48 (top), 54, 70, 90
Ellie Kurttz, summer 2016 production: 6, 10, 18, 20, 24, 26, 28, 30, 32 (left), 38, 42, 44, 48 (bottom), 50, 52, 56, 58, 62 (bottom), 64, 66, 68 (top), 72, 74 (top), 76, 80, 82, 84, 86, 88
Pete Le May: 4

Every effort has been made to trace all copyright holders, but if any have been inadvertently overlooked the Publishers will be pleased to make the necessary arrangements at the first opportunity.

Orders: please contact Bookpoint Ltd, 130 Milton Park, Abingdon, Oxon OX14 4SB.

Telephone: (44) 01235 827720. Fax: (44) 01235 400454. Lines are open 9.00 – 5.00, Monday to Saturday, with a 24-hour message answering service.

Visit our website at www.hoddereducation.co.uk

© The Shakespeare Globe Trust, 2016

First published in 2017 by

Hodder Education,

An Hachette UK Company
Carmelite House
50 Victoria Embankment
London EC4Y 0DZ

Impression number   5 4 3 2 1

Year   2020 2019 2018 2017

All rights reserved. Apart from any use permitted under UK copyright law, no part of this publication may be reproduced or transmitted in any form or by any means, electronic or mechanical, including photocopying and recording, or held within any information storage and retrieval system, without permission in writing from the publisher or under licence from the Copyright Licensing Agency Limited. Further details of such licences (for reprographic reproduction) may be obtained from the Copyright Licensing Agency Limited, Saffron House, 6–10 Kirby Street, London EC1N 8TS.

Cover photograph Stephen Fry as Malvolio (front) and (left to right behind) Colin Hurley as Sir Toby, Roger Lloyd-Pack as Sir Andrew and James Garnon as Fabian, 2012 production, photograph Simon Annand

Typeset in ITC Century Light 10pt by DC Graphic Design Limited, Hextable Village, Kent

Printed in Italy

A catalogue record for this title is available from the British Library

ISBN: 978 1471 89669 9